Foreword by SIG [

MENTORSHIP
MASTERY

A HOLISTIC GUIDE
FOR VIRTUOUS LEADERS

JULIE CAMPBELL

CONTRIBUTING AUTHORS: REAR ADMIRAL PAUL BECKER · KRISTEN DOMBROWSKI
BRUCE ENGELHARDT · JUDY FARRELL · DAVID J. FOSTER · MARK C. GERMANO
KRISTIN A. GOODRICH · CAPT CHUCK HOLLINGSWORTH · DR. MIKE JEFFERSON
ALICEANNE LOFTUS · LORALEI MATISSE · JAMES R McNEAL · CDR JAMES B. MONTGOMERY
KATHY NADO · COLIN PASCAL · ROB SHEPHERD · RENEE SHERWOOD · RAY L. STEINMETZ
CAITRIONA TAYLOR · MARINA TOUW · DONALD W. VINCI · KRISTEN WHITLEY · JEROME ZAZZERA

Foreword by SIG BERG

MENTORSHIP MASTERY

A HOLISTIC GUIDE FOR VIRTUOUS LEADERS

JULIE CAMPBELL

CONTRIBUTING AUTHORS: REAR ADMIRAL PAUL BECKER · KRISTEN DOMBROWSKI
BRUCE ENGELHARDT · JUDY FARRELL · DAVID J. FOSTER · MARK C. GERMANO
KRISTIN A. GOODRICH · CAPT CHUCK HOLLINGSWORTH · DR. MIKE JEFFERSON
ALICEANNE LOFTUS · LORALEI MATISSE · JAMES R McNEAL · CDR JAMES B. MONTGOMERY
KATHY NADO · COLIN PASCAL · ROB SHEPHERD · RENEE SHERWOOD · RAY L. STEINMETZ
CAITRIONA TAYLOR · MARINA TOUW · DONALD W. VINCI · KRISTEN WHITLEY · JEROME ZAZZERA

Mentorship Mastery
A Holistic Guide for Virtuous Leaders

Copyright © 2025 Julie Campbell

Published by Brave Healer Productions

Designed by Dino Marino Design, dinomarinodesign.com

Paperback ISBN: 978-1-961493-88-9

eBook ISBN: 978-1-961493-89-6

"*Mentorship Mastery* offers both inspiring stories and practical strategies ranging from an introduction to the Severn Leadership Group's core virtues and practices to advanced insights on mentoring techniques and philosophies. This book provides an intimate exploration of relationship building and shows how a culture of mentoring can strengthen the fabric of a team or organization. Real-world examples supporting those launching careers, overcoming setbacks, fostering family and community ties, and growing as leaders illustrate why holistic mentoring can have a profoundly positive impact on lives. The 25 chapters combine to build a formidable iceberg of holistic mentorship guidance. Only the readers will begin to see what is under the water as they serve as mentors to others."

**- Mike Murphy, Partner, Educational Directions,
SLG Virtual Program Manager**

"*Mentorship Mastery* is an excellent collection of stories on holistic mentoring from many outstanding leaders. The stories will make you laugh, cry, and stand in awe at some of the many ways to be a great holistic mentor. Today's world needs virtuous leaders, and the best way to create a virtuous leader is through mentoring. Whether you're a mentor or a leader with a desire to mentor, this book will greatly help your journey."

**- Joe Fougere,
Retired Engineering Director and Executive Project Manager**

"This book is a powerful tribute to the mentoring we give and receive throughout our lives. It's brimming with moving stories, practical tools, and timeless lessons on leadership and the art of transformative mentorship from experts who lead with both heart and knowledge."

- Elizabeth Harris, MS, RDN, Certified Intuitive Eating Counselor

---

"*Mentorship Mastery* is a rich, multi-voiced guide to the art and impact of mentorship. With contributions from seasoned leaders, the book blends personal stories, practical strategies, and timeless wisdom. It offers mentors a thoughtful framework for fostering growth, trust, and transformation. A must-read for anyone seeking to mentor with depth, authenticity, and purpose."

- Jennifer A. Rayno, NPH USA, VP Donor Relations

"Julie Campbell masterfully assembled an esteemed cadre of mentors to share their pilgrimage to help others reach a goal despite challenges and doubt. Their adroit application of active listening, encouragement, goal setting, and no judgment created an environment of trust, which contributed to success. The common purpose of SLG is on full display in this collaborative book. Inspiring and conjures up the leadership values of icons like Lincoln and Jefferson: lead while being led, persuade rather than coerce, honesty and integrity, and common purpose leads to unity of effort. A must-read."

- Mario F Montero Jr. MG US Army (Ret.), VP, Defense Systems Engineering

---

"In *Mentorship Mastery*, Julie Campbell masterfully compiles diverse leadership perspectives, creating a compelling read. Through powerful short stories and insightful prompts, the book encourages introspection and broadens our understanding of leading with integrity, courage, and humility. It's an essential resource for anyone on the rewarding journey of mentorship, especially those who are called to lead and serve!"

- Graig D. Paglieri, Chief Executive Randstad Digital, USMC Infantry Captain 1994-1999

"As a member of the Severn Leadership Group, I've had the honor to serve with most of the authors of Mentorship Mastery. The common thread between these successful mentors is their ability to recognize and harness the power of vulnerability, skillfully employ questions, and avoid the temptation to solve mentee problems. Savor this treasure trove of insights and reflections from those with first-hand experiences leading organizational change, dealing with adversity, and enabling individuals to flourish."

- Col Ray Rottman, USAF (ret), Executive Director, Association of Military Colleges and Schools of the United States (AMCSUS) and SLG Annapolis Program Manager

---

"This book is filled with advice and stories that provide excellent insights and reminders about the power and importance of mentoring and being mentored. It is also a pervasive testimony to the spiritual circle of gratitude and love that fuels so much of the mentoring relationship."

- Sheldon Church, SLG Mentor and Board Member

"Reading *Mentorship Mastery* was inspiring and practical. The stories are real, heartfelt, and reminded me of the mentors who shaped my own personal journey. What I appreciated most was how each chapter blended personal experience with lessons I can use right away in my own leadership and mentoring. It's not just a book about leading—it's about walking beside others with courage, integrity, and compassion. I came away encouraged and motivated to be more intentional as a mentor. A truly meaningful read."

- VADM T. J. Benedict, USN (Ret.), President, Systems Planning and Analysis

---

"*Mentorship Mastery* is a beautiful compilation of heartfelt stories and thoughts centered on growing the inner potential within ourselves and those in our circles of influence and care. There are pearls of wisdom for truly anyone. I felt empowered to be a better leader to my children, employees, patients, and friends after reading. You could revisit it many times, and something new will reverberate with you each time."

**- Chris Anderson, DDS, FAGD,
Owner of Annapolis Family Dentistry**

"*Mentorship Mastery: A Holistic Guide for Virtuous Leaders* is a collection of stories and strategies from 24 mentors who emphasize character, courage, and authentic connection with others. Drawing on personal experiences across military, business, education, and faith communities, the book highlights holistic mentoring that drives the development of the whole person. It blends practical tools with inspiring narratives, showing how mentors shape leaders through presence, trust, and integrity, ultimately fostering true transformation in individuals, teams, and organizations. A powerful and worthwhile read."

- Bill Mohl, Senior Executive and Board Member

"A fantastic resource for both new and experienced mentors. This is a well-conceived combination of powerful vignettes and recipes for successful mentorships. A wide range of contributing authors reflect the breadth and depth of the current workforce, and their input highlights flexibility and improvisation in mentoring styles. A must-read for both those contemplating mentorship as well as those with experience in this symbiotic field."

**- Bret Pasiuk, MD, FASN,
Chief of the Medical Staff, St. Agnes Hospital**

"*Mentorship Mastery: A Holistic Guide for Virtuous Leaders* is an inspiring and practical resource that empowers mentors to lead with intention and purpose. Through authentic stories and actionable strategies, it provides tools to build trust, foster personal and professional growth, and navigate challenges with confidence. Each story is unique and truly powerful, showcasing how a strong mentor has impacted each author's life. This guide blends insight with heart, inspiring readers to forge meaningful connections and become transformative mentors. It's a must-read for those committed to growth and virtuous leadership."

- Lisa Datka, Chief Marketing Officer, Early Learning Academies

---

"Throughout my career and business journey, I've been blessed to be both a mentee and a mentor, and yet I couldn't quite articulate the value both experiences have given me. Through real-life stories and practical strategies, this book gives words to what mentorship means and how it radically transforms the lives and businesses of those who experience it. Whether you're a mentor, mentee, or have wondered how mentorship can impact your own growth, this book is for you!"

- Erin Harrigan, Christian Business Coach for Women

"I have sent several AMSG team members through Severn Leadership Group's programs, and each one described it as a deeply meaningful experience. *Mentorship Mastery* reflects that same spirit—sharing powerful stories of mentors who lead with courage, humility, and integrity. This book reminds us that mentorship is about presence, listening, and walking beside others to help them find their path. It is an inspiring guide for leaders committed to transformation."

- Jim O'Farrell, President & CEO,
Advanced Management Strategies Group (AMSG)

DEDICATION

To all the Severn Leadership Group Mentors, past, present, and future. Your dedication amazes me. Your humility humbles me. Your wisdom is unsurpassed. You have created a space where our SLG Fellows and all whom you mentor are poured into and thrive. You are changing the trajectory of teams, organizations, communities, and our world, one leader at a time. Well done and thank you!

IN MEMORY

In loving memory of Vice Admiral John T. (Ted) Parker, Jr., U.S. Navy (Ret.), founding member of the Severn Leadership Group—a stalwart mentor to many of us. His memory permeates all we do at SLG.

DISCLAIMER

This book is designed to provide competent, reliable, and educational information regarding mentorship, business growth, and other subject matter covered. However, it is sold with the understanding that the authors and publisher specifically disclaim all responsibility for any liability, loss, or risk, personal or otherwise, incurred as a consequence, directly or indirectly, of the use and application of any of the contents of this publication.

In order to maintain the anonymity of others, the names and identifying characteristics of some people, places, and organizations described in this book have been changed.

This publication contains content that may be potentially triggering or disturbing. Individuals who are sensitive to certain themes are advised to exercise caution while reading.

The opinions, ideas, and recommendations contained in this publication do not necessarily represent those of the Publisher. The use of any information provided in this book is solely at your own risk.

Our authors represent cultures worldwide, and as such, there may be differences in language and expressions. As a global publisher, we have made a conscious choice not to edit these nuances so each chapter is authentic and in its author's words.

Know that the experts here have shared their tools, practices, and knowledge with you with a sincere and generous intent to assist you on your business journey. Please contact them with any questions you may have about the techniques or information they provided. They will be happy to assist you further and be an ongoing resource for your success!

FOREWORD

Few people knew his name. But those who did—truly did—never forgot him. I'm one of them.

Mr. Jonas Segal spoke five languages, served as an international troubleshooter for Hilton Hotels, and in the early 1950s helped repatriate Jewish children from Iran and Russia to Israel. He moved through the world with quiet distinction. And yet, he chose to spend the bulk of his life as a high school teacher in Detroit.

That's where I met him—in his *History of Western Thought* class. We kept in touch over the years. Even as time passed, I could never bring myself to call him Jonas. Out of deep respect, he was always Mr. Segal.

Years later, we met for lunch in Kalamazoo, Michigan—halfway between Detroit and Chicago. I was a parish pastor then; he was retired. Our four-hour conversation picked up as if no time had passed. We talked theology—Jewish Scripture and the Gospels. He quoted from memory in Hebrew and Greek. But what struck me most wasn't his intellect—it was his care.

"How are you really doing?" he asked. "What are you struggling with?" "Where is your life headed?"

He asked about my wife, Martha—whom he had also taught—and spoke of her with genuine warmth.

When I asked why he never pursued a university post or a corporate role, his answer was simple: "Because I could make the greatest difference with high school students. And it gave me time with Shiphrah—my wife."

Only later did I connect her name with the Hebrew midwife who defied Pharaoh's order to kill male Hebrew newborns, saving countless lives. Fitting—for two people so quietly devoted to nurturing life, wisdom, and conscience.

Just before we departed that Saturday afternoon, Mr. Segal offered one final piece of advice:

"Your place of greatest influence may not always be at the top. You can accomplish much more flying under the radar."

Our time together felt like I was walking along a wooded path with a trusted guide. He was still mentoring. Still listening. Still urging me forward.

Mr. Segal never pretended life was simple. He spoke honestly about sorrow, injustice, and the brokenness of the world. But he never let it paralyze him. He lived his faith—quietly, steadily, humbly. He knew who he was. And he walked his talk.

In moments of frustration, I still hear his voice—steady, wise, full of hope.

This book carries that same spirit. It honors mentors who show up, stay present, and walk beside others through their most vulnerable moments. They don't seek the spotlight. They plant seeds—quietly, faithfully, and often unseen.

And now, it's your turn. You are needed. Your presence. Your wisdom. Your steady belief in others. You don't need a title or a platform—just the courage to listen, the humility to walk alongside, and the heart to speak hope when it's needed most.

To listen when others feel unheard.

To believe when others lose heart.

To guide with patience, strength, and compassion.

We may never see the full impact of our mentoring. But like Mr. Segal, we can walk our talk. And in doing so, help others find theirs.

The calling of the Severn Leadership Group is to cultivate leaders and their teams to transform our culture.

Mentoring is the linchpin of our process.

This is our invitation—one we are called to answer.

And the time to begin is now.

Sig Berg

Founder, Severn Leadership Group

TABLE OF CONTENTS

PART: 4
ADVANCED TECHNIQUES

INTRODUCTION

Leadership starts with you, but is not about you.

~ Sig Berg

"You need to do this. They need more women, mentors like you. You were made for this," my husband, Chris, encourages me.

Pins and needles. My skin is bursting with excitement, including the tip of my nose. It is my first meeting with the Severn Leadership Group (SLG) Mentors. SLG Founder Sig Berg, a tall, distinguished-looking gentleman, welcomes us with a firm handshake and a warm smile.

Men in suits, sport coats, jeans, Hawaiian T-shirts and shorts, and a few women in dresses, or blazer with jeans–my fellow mentors, from all industries and walks of life, greet me with handshakes and hugs welcoming me on an adventure that will change the leadership journey for me and so many others. A journey of virtuous leadership and mentorship, so profound and powerful that years later, these mentors and those who follow can look back in amazement and awe at something that seemed so simple, has transformed the lives of so many leaders, their families, and their organizations.

We begin with the logistics, receive our materials, a book, a thumb drive of biographies, and a promise.

You will receive more than you give.

Nothing is truer than that.

Over the past ten years, I've had the privilege to learn from all of our selfless mentors, including the 24 mentor authors who had the courage to write a chapter in this special book. Their authentic stories of setbacks, failure, firm foundations, self-awareness, faith, recovery, resilience, and success embody the LITER virtues of love, integrity, truth, excellence, and relationships. They walk the talk of a virtuous leader as they walk alongside those they mentor.

It often sounds something like this…

He doesn't sit in the executive meetings.

His name isn't on the organization chart.

But when the SLG Fellow feels the ground shifting under her, she calls him.

They meet in a quiet coffee shop. No strict agenda.

She vents about two of her team members who are at odds over priorities. Her staff can't move forward, and she is at an impasse.

He doesn't give her a checklist.

He listens. Really listens.

Then he says, "What would it look like if you didn't try to solve it?"

She pauses. A lightbulb moment.

He asks, "What's the story you're telling yourself about what you should control?"

She smiles and looks up, appreciating this sacred moment, a new fire in her eyes.

Back at the office, she begins showing up differently. Less fixer, more facilitator, building up, not breaking down relationships. The team notices. Their behavior changes.

Weeks pass. Her confidence grows, not because he gave her answers—but because he made space for her to find better ones.

She gets promoted again.

He's not at the celebration dinner.

But her remarks are full of his fingerprints.

He never wanted credit.

But he lit the fuse of transformation.

The purpose of the mentor is not to just provide advice or to play the expert, but to walk with you during the process: to help you see yourself clearly within a lived context at the testing point and to encourage you to incrementally level up to achieve the best version of yourself.

~ Sig Berg, *The Virtue Proposition: Five Virtues That Will Transform Leadership, Team Performance, and You*

Mentors are the linchpin to SLG and leading a better life. Leadership (and mentorship) starts with you, but is not about you.

The SLG exists to cultivate a new generation of leaders and followers who embrace timeless and transcendent virtues, empowered to catalyze virtuous transformation in our world. We could not do that without our mentors.

I can't be more excited to share just a piece of who our incredible mentors are, their why, their how, and their impact. I invite you to read through each of our stories and feel encouraged and inspired to mentor with the Severn Leadership Group or wherever you lead and live.

Mentoring holistically is not about the career; it's about the person. Each chapter is steeped in a beautiful story and practical strategy that you can immediately implement as you continue your journey as a holistic mentor. Don't be surprised if you reap the rewards of reverse mentoring, along the way, too. It's worth every second!

PART: 1

THE BUILDING BLOCKS
OF HOLISTIC MENTORING

CHAPTER ONE

WHOLE PERSON MENTORING

CULTIVATING COURAGE, CHARACTER, AND TRANSFORMATION

Julie Campbell, President/CEO, Severn Leadership Group

Mentoring is a fluid process—as a discipline, as the mentor, and for the mentee—all three are changing and growing in real time. Love it, even as I am challenged by it.

~ SLG Mentor

MY STORY

COURAGE

I have been summoned.

"Commander, can you meet me in my office?"

Heart pounding, stomach churning, my boss wants to see me in his office, privately. Let me be more specific. The Commander of the White House Communications Agency wants to speak to me now!

I am a rule follower.

I am the leader of an 80-person Presidential Communications Command composed of soldiers, sailors, airmen, and marines in a high-visibility, zero-defect, critical national security organization. Our mission is to provide secure and emergency communications for the President, Vice President, and First Lady of the United States, both domestically and internationally, while they are away from the White House.

"Close the door. We need to talk."

While I didn't get in trouble that time, I learned how my behavior and the behavior of my team while on a presidential visit to Atlantic City (prior to the President's arrival) could have been perceived as reckless, poor judgment, and certainly not virtuous. I swallowed my humble pill and walked out of his office, enlightened and determined to do better for my team.

Don't worry, nothing scandalous, illegal, or untoward happened on that trip. But if you know me, I enjoy playing a good game of cards. Cha-ching!

COL Howard (Howie) Cohen, USA (Ret.), was my first holistic mentor. As I look back now, most of our long mentor-mentee conversations were about my why, my trajectory, where I saw myself in 5, 10, and 20 years, and what I could do to reach my aspirations. Those conversations were driven by me but guided by a master. Unbeknownst to me at the time, he was instilling in me the virtues that ground us at SLG:

Love, integrity, truth, excellence, relationships (LITER), and courage.

"Do you want to be a speedboat, sailboat, or rowboat?"

What?

While sometimes cryptic, he helped me see things about myself that I had not seen. He gave me the **courage** to do things I never thought I could do (speedboat!). And challenged me to **excellence**, not to just sail through life without a care or row without direction.

"What is under that big rock?

Do I really have to turn it over? You are the leader, Julie — yes, you do!

Find the **truth** in the situation.

"What will you do when you find what's beneath it?" he'd encourage me to think it out loud.

*Do what you say. Practice what you preach and hold others accountable to the standards we have set. Lead with **integrity**.*

And that day, he called me into his office – he taught me about tough **love**.

COL Cohen and I got to know each other through our **relationship of shared purpose**. Our mission was our guiding light. Over time, it became a treasure, a relationship of mutual respect. He was like a big brother, one who changed the trajectory of my life and how I lead today.

CHARACTER

Fast forward three years, and my career in the Navy is coming to a natural end. My why and values are changing. I've met the love of my life. My 5–10-year goals that I shared with COL Cohen:

- *Meet someone (check)*
- *Get married (check)*
- *Start a family…* is happening!

But I still desire to work and make a difference.

What can I do that is meaningful work, is close to our new home, allows me time to support my new husband, is different, and FUN?

Like a kid in a candy store, I do all the things to prepare:

- The Navy's Executive Transition Assistance Program (TAP), where I learn how to write a "civilian" resume.
- Dig into *What Color is Your Parachute*, by Richard N. Bolles, and dream of a job that meets all of my criteria.
- Schedule endless "informational interviews" where I ask thousands of questions of people who appear to have the ideal job.
- Career fair after career fair, I feel like I'm fresh meat at a meat market.

Nothing.

I'm stuck.

"You should talk to Brian, one of the leaders, where I work." One of my Navy colleagues encourages me.

This colleague is a Navy Reservist whose civilian job is at a defense contracting business.

Ugh. That's not different. How can it be FUN?

"They have an office in Annapolis," he says optimistically.

A glimmer of hope. Maybe?

What do I have to lose?

So, I scheduled yet another informational interview with Brian Dewey, Director of Operations at the Defense Systems Engineering and Services Division at ARINC. I don't expect much.

Donning nice slacks, blouse, and heels (*is this what I'm supposed to wear?*), I drive to our neighborhood Panera Bread for the first of many such meetings over the next six months with Brian Dewey.

With butterflies in my stomach, I walk up to the door and see a nicely dressed gentleman, shorter than me (in my heels), with a short gray military haircut, glasses, and smiling eyes. He welcomes me warmly, buys my coffee, and guides me to a table.

"Let's talk!" His enthusiasm is unexpected. It feels different.

Month after month, we met at that Panera. Brian asked question after question and really listened.

"Tell me your life story."

"What are your goals and dreams?"

"Tell me about your family."

"What energizes you?"

"What drags you down?"

As we continued to meet, Brian always started by asking how Chris and I were doing and how my job search was progressing. I would ask him about his boys and what he was working on at work, about his team, their mission (supporting "America's sons and daughters" – the Department of

Defense), and about his boss, the Vice President of the division (a retired Army general).

TRANSFORMATION

And then slowly, the discussions became different.

"What would you do if you were in my shoes?" he quips.

"How would you solve this problem?"

"Tell me what it means to lead?"

And then,

"I'd like you to meet my boss."

The fog was lifting.

Brian was building a relationship of trust. He was mentoring me!

But he was also preparing me for my transition. And helping me find a job that was: meaningful work, close to our new home, allowed me the time to support my new husband, was different, and FUN!

The day came to meet his boss. Dressed in slacks, blazer, and heels, I walked into Panera to be greeted by Brian and Major General Monty Montero, USA (Ret.).

He's SHORTER than me! Why didn't Brian tell me not to wear heels?

I was offered a job the next day, heels and all.

Brian became my boss for the next four years, but that did not stop him from mentoring me and many of the others who worked for and with him.

Every day, he would stop by my desk and check the weather.

"How are things?"

I could go to him for anything.

He supported my decisions.

He challenged all of us, celebrated our successes, provided constructive feedback, and asked for input, new ideas, and feedback on how he was doing, how our VP was doing, and where we could improve as a team. Brian considered his role on "Team Monty" an honor and privilege. As

Monty's right-hand man, he kept the pulse of our business unit. And he did it with humility and grace.

On Saturday, May 7, after a long week at work, something was not quite right.

Was it something I ate?

38 weeks pregnant, I time my contractions.

I think it's time!

On Mother's Day, May 8, 2011, our first son was born.

For what seems like too long, the nurses have him on a high table, under a light, lots of fussing.

Is this what's supposed to happen?

And then we get to hold him—a beautiful, round (*blue*) faced, little boy.

It's not long before the pediatrician comes and sits at the end of my bed.

"I'm sorry. We think your baby has Down syndrome."

No, he doesn't! Look how perfect he is!

The nurses snap a picture. Chris and I, holding our son, were in a state of total shock. It still haunts me.

One of the first calls I make is to Brian.

"I need more time. We must move to the Neonatal Intensive Care Unit (NICU). I don't know what our future holds."

"That's okay. Take the time you need." Brian's voice is soft but firm and oh so reassuring.

He clears my calendar, covers my work, and gets the short-term disability and FMLA paperwork moving. I don't need to worry about a thing at work.

Weeks later, Brian invites us into the office to celebrate our homecoming. He's the first to greet us with tears in his eyes, a long hug, and a handshake.

"Congratulations!"

I want to lead and mentor like Brian.

I want others to be blessed with mentors like Brian.

THE STRATEGY

How does one become a holistic mentor? What is a mentor, anyway?

Mentor, coach, consultant, therapist, and spiritual director, who do you aspire to be?

- **Mentor:** An experienced traveler, walking next to you, helping you navigate your own road.
- **Coach:** A GPS helping you set your destination and reroute when needed, or a trainer who helps develop your skills and reach your potential to navigate the challenges of competition.
- **Consultant:** A mechanic diagnosing and fixing a car.
- **Therapist or Counselor:** A healer helping you understand the old wounds that still hurt.
- **Spiritual Director:** A gentle guide helping you open your mind as you listen for the divine.

My co-authors have chosen the path of mentorship, even though many of them also work in professions such as coaching, consulting, therapy, counseling, and spiritual direction. More specifically, they have chosen the path of holistic mentoring. Holistic mentors focus on the whole person. It's not just about career mentoring, skill mentoring, or faith mentoring. Holistic mentoring is all that and so much more.

It's about walking alongside another to help them see themselves clearly, encouraging their journey, and holding them accountable to achieve the best version of themselves.

It starts with a firm foundation. At the Severn Leadership Group, our holistic mentoring is grounded in a set of virtues that we believe every leader should ascribe to. **LITER + C: love, integrity, truth, excellence,** and **relationship**, catalyzed by **courage**.

At SLG, we mentor leaders who desire to develop their character using these three precepts:

1. Leadership is defined by one's character.
2. Character is shaped by timeless and transcendent virtues.

3. Selfless courage and service to others is not a style of leadership, but a learned behavior.

All serious athletes need a coach to perform at their best, so, too, all serious leaders need a mentor who is personally aligned to these transcendent virtues to call them to the best version of themselves in practice. Serious formation in virtues requires a mentor.

~ Sig Berg, The Virtue Proposition. Five Virtues that Will Transform Leadership, Team Performance, and You.

Consistent mentoring that cultivates courage, character, and transformation across individuals from all industries, walks of life, and experiences requires a systems-based approach to mentoring.

If you'd like to develop mentors for your organization, here's a place to start.

MENTOR CERTIFICATION SYSTEM

Commitment

Your mentors must voice commitment to the organization's mission and to those they will mentor.

Severn Leadership Group mentors are committed to inspiring a fellow to 'live a life of selfless courage and service to others, before self'. Mentors listen, question, encourage, challenge and provide feedback to their fellows. They serve as the face of the Severn Leadership Group, model its perspectives, and 'walk the talk'.

~ Severn Leadership Group Commitment Form

Step 1: Create a mentor commitment form that mentors review and sign annually. It should include specific expectations:

- Roles and responsibilities
- Training required
- Minimum time commitment
- Communication
- Fees or materials required
- Feedback and assessments

Formal Training Certification

The certification should include interviews, a foundation, and a curriculum.

Step 2: When developing your formal certification, must-haves include:

- Interviews for experience, alignment, availability, and most importantly, for character.
  - **Some of the best mentor candidates are referred by other mentors.**

- A foundation grounded in consistent principles or ethos.
  - **At SLG, our foundation is virtue.**

- A robust curriculum that works toward a common goal and includes self-study, instruction, reflection, discussion, observation, and post-certification continuing education.
  - **At SLG, our common goal is virtuous character.**

Community of Practice

Mentors need other mentors.

*The best way to become a virtuous leader is
to surround yourself with other virtuous leaders.*

~ SLG Mentor

Step 3: Cultivate a strong and dedicated community.

As a new mentor in an organization, it is the experienced mentors who surround them as they navigate the "system." Consider assigning a sponsor for new mentors. A sponsor is a mentor who has successfully mentored in your organization and can be another sounding board for the mentor in training.

Consider employing regular check-ins, mentor gatherings, surveys, two-way feedback sessions, accountability partners, celebrations, and opportunities for mentors to become trainers and facilitators.

And don't forget **gratitude**. Celebrate sharing precious time together.

Why mentors?

Developing mentors to develop leaders amplifies our mission at SLG to develop and support leaders and teams to be catalysts of transformational change.

Our mentors deeply care for the mission and the mentoring they do.

The SLG approach to the mentoring process has brought tremendous clarity...and structure to what was a tangle of long-held and important ideas and concepts. Above all, understanding the role and importance of courage has had a profound personal and professional impact.

~ Sheldon Church, SLG Mentor and Chairman of the Board

Do you want to transform the culture of your organization? Consider adopting a culture of mentoring. It will do more than transform your culture. It will perpetuate well-being in the world.

Julie Campbell, President and CEO of the Severn Leadership Group (SLG), is making the world a better place through virtuous leadership. She is the mother of two strong-willed boys and the wife and head cheerleader for her college athletics coaching husband and his team. She served for 20 years in the U.S. Navy, holding various leadership positions in space systems, electronic warfare, and communications, followed by 15 years of leadership experience in the defense, information technology, and nonprofit industries. With a passion and curiosity for people and their purposes, Julie is a lifelong mentor and collaborator with a mission to help others level up their leadership as they change the world.

When she is not knee-deep in creating partnerships, fundraising, writing, and growing the SLG network of mentors, fellows, and supporters, you can find her volunteering at her son's school, shuttling her boys to sports, playing board games, or walking, listening to podcasts, and reading (sometimes all three at once)!

Join Julie at SLG and level up your leadership with virtue, emotional intelligence, and grace.

Connect with Julie:

Email: julie.campbell@severnleadership.org

LinkedIn: https://www.linkedin.com/in/campbell-juliem/

SLG Website: https://www.severnleadership.org

SLG LinkedIn: https://www.linkedin.com/company/severnleadershipgroup

SLG Facebook: https://www.facebook.com/severnleadershipgroup

SLG Instagram: https://www.instagram.com/slg_org/

SLG YouTube: https://www.youtube.com/@severnleadershipgroup8168

We Lead: Building Connection, Community, and Collaboration for WOMEN IN BUSINESS with Lead Author AliceAnne Loftus: https://a.co/d/ajUD4FM

We Lead: Building Connection, Community, and Collaboration for WOMEN IN BUSINESS (Vol 2) with Lead Author AliceAnne Loftus: https://a.co/d/6ssjEEf

CHAPTER TWO

HOLISTIC MENTORSHIP THROUGH CHANGE

YOUR COMPASS WHEN THE PATH IS UNCLEAR

Marina Touw

MY STORY

I'm in the sweet spot in my career, my future is coming into focus, and I'm walking away from it.

I had no idea what to do.

Rather, I knew what I wanted to do, but I didn't know how to do it.

I'm a Surface Warfare Officer (SWO) in the Navy and was on the same career path for 10 years when I decided I wanted to take a leap of faith and make a major career change. This wasn't a decision I took lightly. My entire professional life was dedicated to preparing me for the ultimate goal of a SWO: commanding a warship at sea.

Along the way, I was blessed with some incredible mentors. Most were fellow SWOs who invested their time because they saw promise in me. It feels pretty good to hear someone say, "Hey, I'm going to dedicate time to training you because I think you have what it takes to have a long and successful career in this community." *Awesome. Sign me up.*

I loved my job. I loved being a SWO and going out to sea, and I especially loved the people I worked with. I weighed all these factors against my desire to change course and apply for a program that would take me off the traditional SWO path. I knew in my heart exactly what I wanted to do, but it was a hard decision to make.

Step one was to talk to my Executive Officer (XO), my direct supervisor. I was anxious about talking to him about pursuing my passion to be a permanent military instructor at the U.S. Naval Academy. My XO was an incredible mentor for me and always encouraged me to reach my full potential. I trusted his input and respected his advice. However, I was afraid he would be disappointed in my decision, viewing my change of heart as a failure—not just on my part, but on his as well. After pouring so much time and energy into preparing me to thrive in our field, I feared leaving would render all of it meaningless. I knew I would be a letdown.

I couldn't be more wrong.

I sat in front of my boss and told him my plan. I explained why I wanted to make the change, what excited me about the new opportunity, and what would be hard to leave behind. When I finished, I braced to defend my answer and waited for him to start trying to convince me I was misguided.

Instead, he asked, "How can I help?"

OUR HUMAN NEED FOR CONNECTION

It's our human nature to desire clarity. We want to know where we're headed, and we're on that path for a unique and important purpose. We long to be known, heard, cared for, championed, and supported. The deeper connection that comes with being understood is at the core of holistic mentorship.

Holistic mentorship goes beyond transactional advice or guidance. It's vulnerable. It requires a willingness to share one's thoughts, aspirations, and shortcomings. It calls for authenticity, as both the mentor and mentee are engaged in a relationship of mutual trust and respect. This depth is what makes mentorship both profoundly rewarding and incredibly challenging.

Holistic mentorship proves especially powerful during times of change, transition, and uncertainty. These are precisely the moments when mentorship is most needed. All too often, the chaos and complexity of the situation tend to overwhelm our ability to step back and see the bigger picture. In my own experience, when life becomes overwhelming or competing demands pile up, my instinct is to tighten my grip and try to manage everything on my own. I've had to learn the value of reaching out for support. This is far more difficult than it sounds. It takes humility, vulnerability, and a deep level of trust.

When my boss responded with, "How can I help?" I was taken aback. It took a moment before I realized: *I don't have to do this alone.*

As a holistic mentor, you can also have a profound impact on others—and you're not alone on this journey.

THE STRATEGY

Holistic mentorship during times of transition and change is powerful for several key reasons:

- **Broadens perspective.** A mentor offers fresh insight and alternative viewpoints, helping the mentee see the bigger picture and make sense of complex circumstances.

- **Clarifies purpose.** Mentors guide their mentees in uncovering the deeper "why" behind their transition, anchoring them in a sense of purpose amid uncertainty.

- **Initiates a shared journey**. Rather than standing on the sidelines, effective mentors walk alongside their mentees, navigating the twists, turns, and unknowns together. The impact of having someone present on the journey can't be overstated.

To embrace this practice as a holistic mentor, there are three key principles to remember: engage, listen, and champion.

ENGAGE

My XO had an uncanny ability to stop whatever he was doing and give his full attention to whoever walked through his office door. Whether it was a senior advisor or the most junior member of the crew, he would stop what he was doing and invest in the conversation. This never ceased to amaze me, and I was convinced he had some ability to control the space-time continuum to make time for everyone and continue to excel at his job.

Time-warping mysteries aside, when I stopped by his office to talk about my big plans for a career shift, he once again put everything aside and gave me his full attention. He heard everything I had to say without jumping in or interrupting. He could read the genuine passion I had for this change, and his immediate response was one of support: "This is awesome. How can I help?"

For holistic mentorship to be a transformative experience, the mentor must first choose to fully engage. This begins by showing up with curiosity and a genuine focus on your mentee.

Here are some practical ways to demonstrate you're leaning into the mentorship relationship and ready to engage in a meaningful conversation:

- **Remove distractions.** In a world filled with constant notifications and competing priorities, presence is a rare and powerful gift. Silence your phone, ignore the buzz on your smartwatch, and close your laptop. Create an environment where your mentee has your full attention.

- **Center yourself.** Take a moment to pause and prepare. This could mean a few deep breaths, a short meditation, or reviewing notes from your last session. Preparing yourself and the environment with intention sets the tone for a deeper, more meaningful exchange.

- **Show up early.** Sometimes mentorship happens organically, like a quick office drive-by or casual check-in. However, if you've arranged a meeting, ensure you show up on time, or early if possible. This will give you time to settle in and prepare yourself to be fully present in the mentorship space.

- **Choose a neutral space.** Whenever possible, meet outside the office. A coffee shop or park is a great option. You can take your mentorship on the move and go for a walk. Light movement is a great way to ease tension, foster openness, and stimulate thought and reflection.

- **Ask powerful questions.** As the conversation unfolds, ask powerful questions that challenge your mentee to think more broadly and deeply. Meaningful questions reflect genuine curiosity and enable you and your mentee to gain deeper insights. Especially during periods of change or uncertainty, a mentor's questions can illuminate the real issues at play and guide the mentee toward clarity. Focus on asking open-ended, specific questions that invite reflection rather than simple "yes" or "no" answers.

- **Be intentional and specific.** Tailor your guidance to the mentee's unique context. Avoid generic advice and avoid making assumptions. Don't presume you know where the conversation is headed. Instead, ask clarifying follow-ups that dig deeper and help uncover the core of the matter.

- **Engage selflessly.** Enter the conversation without an agenda. Your goal is to serve the mentee, not to solve everything or prove your expertise. While personal stories can be valuable, use them sparingly and only when they serve the mentee's growth.

Effective mentorship requires the humility to lean in, the patience to listen deeply, and the discernment to speak with intention. As a mentor, you have the unique ability to provide perspective and help your mentee see their situation from different angles and in the context of the larger picture. It's easy to get fixated on one part of a challenge or decision, or limit ourselves to our own vantage point. As a mentor, it's crucial to help clarify the full picture. To do this effectively, you must engage wholeheartedly and with a spirit of selflessness. This will enable a connection that will make all the difference.

LISTEN

After I shared my plan, my XO asked a few questions, then sat back and truly listened. I'd become so accustomed to people trying to talk me into their way of thinking that I was pleasantly surprised to have my boss sincerely want to hear my perspective. What's more, he made it clear he listened to understand rather than to convince me to change my mind.

When I reflected on that moment, I realized something powerful: when you ask good questions, listen intently to the responses, and give people the space to discover the answers on their own, you can transform lives. We've all encountered people who rush to tell us what to do.

"You should do this."

"If I were you…"

But we don't seek out mentorship to be talked at by someone. We come to be listened to and understood. As a mentor, after you show up and ask the questions, it's time to listen.

Active listening is more than staying silent while someone speaks. It's an intentional skill that requires presence, humility, and full engagement. When practiced well, it builds trust, deepens connection, and creates a safe space for the mentee to explore their thoughts openly.

Here are a few ways to strengthen your active listening practice:

- **Be aware of your body language.** Your physical posture speaks volumes. Face your mentee, maintain a relaxed and open posture, and make consistent eye contact to show that you're fully engaged. These small details go a long way to communicate you're listening.

- **Use non-verbal cues.** Small gestures, like nodding or leaning in slightly, signal attentiveness and encourage the speaker to continue. These cues indicate, "I hear what you're saying," and can encourage your mentee to say more.

- **Reflect and rephrase.** Summarize key points in your own words. After your mentee has expressed some thoughts and insight, rephrase the key points back to them. This purpose is twofold. First, it ensures you understood what they were trying to communicate as they intended. Second, when we hear our ideas repeated back to us, it can bring the main points into focus and provide clarity to our thoughts and words.

- **Ask follow-up questions.** Go deeper by asking clarifying or expanding questions. Now that you have some understanding of the situation your mentee wants to discuss, ask more pointed, open-ended questions and allow your mentee to look at the scenario from a different vantage point. By helping your mentee explore different dimensions of their situation, you'll help them draw important connections and extract game-changing lessons.

- **Stay flexible.** Be willing to pivot. The conversation may unfold in unexpected directions. Follow it with curiosity, not control. As you listen actively to your mentee's responses, be flexible. Be willing to adapt, to challenge the person you're mentoring when necessary, and to celebrate their victories along the way. Stay rooted in the moment and allow the conversation to unfold naturally.

Mentorship demands flexibility. People grow in unexpected ways and at different paces. A mentor who is rigid or fixed in their approach may inadvertently stifle growth. Mentorship isn't about telling someone what to do; it's about being present, offering support, and knowing when to step in and when to step back. Listening may seem simple, but it is the complex connective tissue that defines the strength of the mentorship. *How* you listen shapes how you engage and how you champion your mentee.

CHAMPION

Believe in your mentee! After my conversation with the XO, he consistently followed up with questions to learn more about the instructor program, celebrated me when I was selected, and supported me through the transition. Although I was branching out and away from my original career path, I never felt abandoned during the process. To this day, he continues to periodically check in, letting me know I'm not alone on this new path.

It's important to be the one who believes in your mentee even when they doubt themselves, when their motivation falters, or when they lose focus on their goals. Championing them consistently has a positive long-term effect as you keep their potential at the forefront.

To build this kind of trust and impact, focus on these five key actions:

- **Connect.** Prioritize authentic connection from the start. Take time to understand who your mentee is, what they value, and what drives them. This foundation fosters openness and psychological safety.

- **Support.** When your mentee feels overwhelmed, show up with empathy and encouragement. Your steady presence can help them regain confidence and focus.

- **Challenge.** Growth doesn't happen in comfort. Invite your mentee to stretch beyond what's familiar. Offer constructive feedback and ask the tough questions.

- **Follow up**. Don't let conversations fade into the background. Revisit goals, check in on progress, and demonstrate your ongoing investment in their development, not just a one-time interaction.

- **Celebrate.** Acknowledge and affirm progress, whether it's a major milestone or a small but significant step forward. Celebration reinforces a sense of achievement and keeps momentum alive.

Mentorship is most impactful when it's consistent, intentional, and grounded in belief. When a mentee feels truly seen, supported, and challenged, they're far more likely to take bold steps forward, even when the path is uncertain. To make this a reality, invest in meaningful connections from the beginning. Offer support when they feel overwhelmed and challenge them when they're complacent. Be proactive in following up, showing your interest and investment are not fleeting but enduring. Celebrate milestones—both big and small—to reinforce the value of the mentorship relationship.

DIFFERENCE MAKERS

I've experienced firsthand the effect of positive mentorship. I've seen the difference it makes when someone engages fully, listens intently and selflessly, and champions endlessly.

As I stepped away from the traditional SWO career path, my XO's support didn't just prepare me for the transition; it inspired me to finish strong. I approached my final months onboard with renewed purpose and a deeper commitment to the team around me. That's the power of holistic mentorship: it not only equips but uplifts. Holistic mentorship can inspire a renewed sense of purpose and re-energize dedication.

Holistic mentorship isn't about having all the answers or a perfect solution for your mentee. It's about engaging sincerely, listening intently, and committing yourself to championing your mentee throughout their journey. This means believing in them when they doubt themselves and walking alongside them despite challenges, uncertainty, and change.

As you commit to growing as a mentor, remember you're not alone. Surround yourself with mentors who challenge, support, and inspire you. Build your network to receive guidance and inspire growth. When we invest in each other, we all rise.

Marina Touw is a Surface Warfare Officer in the U.S. Navy and currently serves as a Permanent Military Instructor of Leadership at the U.S. Naval Academy in Annapolis, Maryland. Originally from Williamsburg, Virginia, Marina grew up in a family where service wasn't just a value, it was a way of life that was ingrained from a young age.

After graduating from the Naval Academy in 2013, Marina began her career with two tours aboard USS Carney (DDG 64), based in Mayport, Florida, and was later forward deployed to Rota, Spain. Her time at sea deepened her commitment to leadership and mentorship, leading her back to Annapolis to pursue the Leadership Education and Development (LEAD) master's program. She earned her M.A. in Leadership and Education from George Washington University and went on to serve as a Company Officer and Executive Assistant to the Commandant of Midshipmen.

Following her time at USNA, she returned to sea duty for two tours aboard USS Zumwalt (DDG 1000) out of San Diego, California, and Pascagoula, Mississippi.

In June 2024, Marina married her husband, Kevin, and the two now call Annapolis home. She finds deep purpose in helping shape the next generation of naval leaders, bringing both operational experience and a passion for mentorship to the classroom and beyond.

Connect with Marina:

LinkedIn: https://www.linkedin.com/in/marina-touw-nanartowich-844900140/

CHAPTER THREE

FAITH AND STORYTELLING

THE FOUNDATIONS OF MENTORING

Kathy J. Nado

I've worked with and for the National Aeronautics and Space Administration (NASA) for over three decades, and storytelling is definitely part of the NASA culture. Faith and storytelling have had an outsized impact on my life, both as a mentor and lifelong learner. My strong faith is a very important element in my approach as a mentor. I am highly motivated to help people identify and conquer obstacles or constraints.

I use faith as my basis for helping others achieve their goals, and I couple faith and storytelling—with lessons learned—as I continue to grow in my role managing and leading people. Finally, I use storytelling as a tool for mentoring and to connect and build relationships.

MY STORY

"Why are you interested in my opinion?" I asked my mentor, Joe. "I'm two decades your junior, and I don't have a technical (engineering) degree."

"When you ask questions, you're trying to grow, to understand," Joe said. "When you give me your insights, there's nothing in it for you.

You're not trying to build an empire; you're just trying to help me deliver on NASA's missions."

I had the remarkable opportunity to work with one of NASA's strongest leaders, Joe Rothenberg, from late 1993 to 2001. From 1993 through today, Joe has mentored, tested, and supported me, while teaching me many life lessons.

I first supported Joe during the operations to repair the Hubble Space Telescope (HST) during the STS-63 Space Shuttle mission in 1993. STS-63 was the culmination of a multi-year effort to develop a technical approach for astronauts to install a "contact lens" on the HST while it operated 270 miles above Earth. By December 1993, it was perceived that the future of NASA hinged on this mission's success, which culminated in restoring HST's ability as one of the premier scientific observatories in the world.

Joe demonstrated great faith in my ability to gather, prioritize, and reshape information as I developed messages to the public during the mission. This was my first experience with a mentor, and it allowed me to build deeper faith in my ability to help our mission succeed.

When Joe provided specific feedback, I was able to develop and refine my skill in leading and managing teams, often in areas where I did not have deep experience. When my confidence would falter, Joe would remind me, "I'm here to ensure that you have the tools and support you need to succeed. Your role is to give your best, learn all you can, lead with faith, humility, and confidence, and ensure that your team delivers for NASA's mission. That is all I ask for." As a result, his faith in my ability propelled me to roles that I would never have dreamed of.

In 1995, Joe became the Center Director of the Goddard Space Flight Center in Maryland, and he asked me to provide insights and lead the development of center-wide messages during a massive reorganization. Getting the opportunity to question the process and help shape the messages—and ultimately the Center's new strategic approach—was a massive leap of faith by Joe in my ability to support him as the Center Director. This is when I first recognized that taking leaps of faith, while leaning on your community, was necessary for growth.

In one instance, while Joe was leading a strategy session about the reorg with his leadership team, a senior woman commented, "How can we expect to effectively lead change if we can't describe the reason why we are changing?" This immediately resonated with me, and I stood up to agree with her that, as leaders, we had been focusing on the "how," but we hadn't agreed on the "why." This is where faith in the ability to articulate – scope and describe – why you are doing something becomes the foundation for the process that will help you and your team move forward.

In 1998, Joe challenged me to course-correct and manage the congressional and public relations activities for NASA's Human Space Flight organization, primarily focusing on the Space Shuttle and International Space Station programs. I inherited a fractured and disconnected approach to developing messages for Congress and the public, and led the development and execution of an integrated communications team that continued to effectively advocate for NASA's budget well after I left in 2001.

With every opportunity I had to lead, Joe mentored me, first as a boss, then as a confidante and friend. When I finally became conscious that he was truly invested in my learning and growing—personally as well as professionally—I started to have faith in my abilities to lead and serve.

Joe mentored me with great sincerity, demonstrated a deep sense of faith in me personally, and gave me the tools to have the courage to accept reality, even when it was disappointing.

Having such a strong leader as a mentor enabled me to have faith in my ability to step up and bring the same gifts to others, both at work and in my personal life. I developed a focus on mentoring as one of my primary means of serving others.

THE STRATEGY

Based on annual civil servant surveys across the U.S. government, NASA has been rated the "Best Place to Work" for 12 straight years. NASA has an awesome mission, phenomenal leadership, and a culture that sincerely embraces celebrating achievements and milestones, no matter how big or small. NASA leadership and extensive training resources reinforce the vital importance of including storytelling as a tool when passing on insights or mentoring someone eager for your guidance, knowledge, and perspectives. NASA recognizes—and I can personally attest—that using storytelling as a tool when mentoring provides an invaluable framework and context to answer almost any question, challenge, or difficult situation.

STORYTELLING

Through the give-and-take of telling a story and directly relating that story to an issue or concern, a mentor can provide layers of nuance to help explain the details and reinforce information that lead to lessons learned.

What was the last story you heard? Was it "remembering" a great vacation when you viewed a photograph? Or perhaps responding to the question "Do you remember where you were when...?" I suspect that when you asked about a photo or responded to a question, sometimes a story followed. Every person has a comfort level with sharing certain parts of themselves, and some people are more comfortable sharing through stories. The same is true with organizations. Focused storytelling, as well as demonstrating honesty and sincerity, is a fundamental element in building relationships. Using this approach, you can lay the foundation of a sincere relationship that supports successful mentoring.

One of the best approaches is for both the mentor and student to sit down, give thanks, and break bread, thus building a personal rapport. If you listen closely, ask thoughtful questions, and take great notes, you will be presented with a wealth of insightful ideas. I've found that if you're focused and your interest is sincere, truly successful people are generous in sharing their ideas, experiences, and stories. Through those experiences, you have all the opportunity in the world to grow.

GOALS AND ACCOUNTABILITY

It's also important to develop a common goal or end state for your mentoring engagements. One of my favorite questions is not, "What is your goal?" but, "How do you measure success—how do *you know* you're making progress toward attaining your goal?" Fleshing out the various layers of what success looks like is a wonderful teaching opportunity, one full of chances to sincerely lead, build faith in competence, and gently challenge the status quo. Ultimately, unless people can identify and resonate with making measurable progress, they'll physically or mentally check out.

Like Joe, many leaders honestly enjoy the opportunity to mentor people who are focused on improving their performance at work and growing as an individual. "I can get an engineering opinion from any number of people," Joe said, "but even lacking a technical degree, your insights are often on point. Your diverse background ensures you look at a problem differently, and I respect that you have your own process."

When a mentor consistently supports *you*, your goals and aspirations, you'll learn valuable life skills and demonstrate personal growth. That's why developing and maintaining faith in your own skills and capabilities is so important, as well as having faith in the sincere effort your mentor is making to help you achieve your goals. In my experience, if someone requests mentoring, they're either entering or embracing a mindset of lifelong learning and personal growth.

KNOWING YOUR VALUES

Fundamentally, it's essential for both the mentor and the student to know their values. This alignment occurs when you sit down and share your thoughts and concerns with each other, both formally and informally. I've discovered you can best help those you mentor pursue their goals if their values align with your own. My values are primarily faith, integrity, service, growth, and compassion (e.g., love when translated to personal life).

Ultimately, sincerity, faith, and focus are the foundation of the approach that I bring when I mentor others, since you can't effectively mentor others if you aren't demonstrating your sincere self. One of NASA's cultural cornerstones is that leaders solicit and accept diverse opinions. And boy, are there stories to tell that reinforce that statement!

USING STORYTELLING TO NAVIGATE CHANGES

Using storytelling is a great opportunity for a mentor to navigate through and around tough subjects. Being exposed to or reading about great leadership qualities, ideas, and skills isn't the same as embracing or practicing these qualities. Both parties should engage in assessing what's needed vs. what the other party can provide—with the end goal in mind. There are both linear and non-linear approaches to balancing the relationship, all of which should ensure psychological safety. Additionally, agreeing on how to measure success within the mentoring relationship is a key step forward. Mentoring discussions should focus on actions that reinforce and promote learning and growth, and enable dialogue on tough subjects, which can be challenging in any relationship.

For myself, I can always relate a mentoring lesson to my experience when NASA's finest astronauts were servicing HST, upgrading the spacecraft so that the science community could reveal new, groundbreaking insights on our universe. Or maybe when I was leading a team focused on advocating to Congress and the American public for an annual budget so NASA can keep astronauts healthy enough to perform the scientific exploration and technological demonstrations that will propel humans deeper into space. During each of these personal and professional growth experiences, I had to have faith. I had to trust in my abilities to lead and serve the team, NASA, and the American public, while also demonstrating faith in the capabilities of my team members.

NASA defines mentoring as: "An active and sincere effort designed to develop the full potential of an individual through the sharing of knowledge, skills, and organizational insight. Mentoring has been identified as a critical component in helping [NASA employees] prepare for and transition to more significant leadership roles." In my experience, both providing and receiving mentoring, mentors offer lessons and insights on the unwritten rules and how to navigate organizational landscapes. These lessons serve as a roadmap for culture—small, large, local, and global—and can aid in successfully navigating the potholes along life's highway. While the experiences we bring to a mentor-mentee relationship are rich fodder to use as a navigation tool during mentoring, the stories we tell are the filter through which we read life's maps.

Many successful mentors balance the following key roles: sounding board, navigator, teacher, and challenger. All these roles must embrace an approach where open communication between both parties is natural and organic.

I like to start discussions with an open question, such as "Would you share the biggest 'win' you've experienced since we last met?" or "What has been the biggest obstacle or 'oops' you have experienced or seen recently?" It is infinitely easier to navigate a discussion based on your mentee's personal observation or experiences than it is to talk in the abstract.

IMPORTANCE OF DEMONSTRATING FAITH IN MENTOR-MENTEE RELATIONSHIP

I've had the great privilege and honor of mentoring a number of members of the military, from the U.S. Air Force, Navy, and Marine Corps to the U.S. Space Force. Almost all my military members have a deep, abiding faith: faith in a greater being, faith in their service to America, and faith in their teammates. However, not all of them have initially demonstrated deep faith in themselves and their capabilities. As a mentor, I gently guide them to look deep into themselves, sometimes at a level that makes them uncomfortable.

My goal as their mentor is to build, then continually reinforce, my mentees' foundation of faith in themselves. I provide them with tools to overcome adversity and maintain a focus on my responsibility to validate them when they articulate their goals. Finally, I reinforce their stated goals when they encounter a setback, refocusing their attention on positive ways to overcome hurdles and get to that goal.

I even occasionally, sincerely questioned their faith in their plan (or lack thereof) and pushed them to develop a contingency or backup plan when they don't believe developing one is necessary. Conceptualizing that they need a backup plan equates to acknowledging that they might not succeed at their baseline plan, and that can be daunting. This was a lesson learned at NASA, where we often develop a list of problems or obstacles, and then our responses to overcome them.

One early career person I mentored had the next 20 years of her career fully mapped out. I asked her, "And what is your contingency plan?" She replied, "I don't need one, I'm a top contender to be hired for this new position; I'm good.". I encouraged her to broaden her view, take her skills, and expand her capabilities into an adjacent career path. When the offer for the new position was put on hold, she was positioned so that she could pursue a different career, based on her contingency planning and interests.

Working with someone and helping them acknowledge not everything will always play out how they planned can be a challenging activity, but the results are always enlightening and measurable. The end result is that someone can recognize they're taking concrete steps toward a solution, overcoming the obstacles that inevitably spring up in their path, and taking steps that will help them attain personal or professional goals.

A characteristic I've seen and personally push back against is when someone who wants to be mentored is looking for a quick solution. As a mentor, I have to have a sincere desire to help, but there's also the responsibility to set the relationship's tone and expectations. It's vital that a mentor can assess the overall capabilities and, concurrently, have a high level of confidence that the person requesting assistance will openly and faithfully participate in the process.

It's truly a mentor's function to ensure someone has the confidence to rise above inner doubts or fears. Mentors can do this by offering guidance and tools to set goals, as well as helping to identify stretch goals. Finally, it's good practice to present and discuss various approaches to measuring progress toward goals, aligned with concrete and achievable timelines.

We've all experienced setbacks; some could characterize a setback as a failure. Faith unequivocally helped me overcome bumps along my path, and as a strong mentor, Joe consistently demonstrated faith in me and my abilities. I came to realize he would always back me up with insights, stories, and actions. That simple declaration of his faith in my abilities and my confidence in the fact that he would help me get back up and brush me off if I suffered a setback, pushed me to develop more fully as a person and as a leader.

USING STORYTELLING TO BALANCE GOALS AND TOOLS

Over the past 20 years, I've mentored peers and subordinates at NASA and through the Severn Leadership Group. I discovered that when someone prematurely ends the formal mentorship program (or if it's an informal interaction, quits participating), it's because the interaction is no longer meeting their needs. To mitigate this, one approach is to intersperse one-on-one meetings with participation in an informal group mentoring session. When you expand mentoring beyond one-on-one, the use of storytelling must be carefully managed, or the value can decline. I've found beginning with the end in mind, utilizing a common definition of success, and being able to provide additional context increases the value of a group interaction.

Interestingly, research acknowledges a balance between experience (having a roadmap) and culture (having the tools to read the roadmap) exists in many successful customer-oriented organizations. In so many organizations, as in life, experience is valuable. One of the hardest lessons to learn is realizing, "What you don't know, you don't know," can delay or even destroy progress. To ensure that the realization of this life lesson doesn't come back to haunt you, a mentor can balance discussing life tools and roadmaps by utilizing storytelling.

In the final equation, the ability to demonstrate faith, to sincerely help someone rise above their inner doubts and fears, and to use appropriate storytelling to provide the framework and context can enable a fruitful and long-lasting relationship. My life experiences have proven that when a mentoring relationship develops beyond the transactional phase into a true friendship, that is a beautiful outcome and an excellent measure of success for all parties involved.

Kathy J. Nado is an experienced government and not-for-profit leader. Her focus is on mentoring the next generation of leaders and followers, and helping individuals and organizations define goals and develop plans that enable them to excel. Kathy returned to NASA headquarters in 2009, where she led efforts as diverse as managing partnerships, leading strategic planning for human spaceflight, and managing performance of extending human presence beyond low Earth orbit; she retired from government service in January 2026.

While detailed from NASA to the Office of Management and Budget (OMB) in 2015, Kathy led the oversight of performance activities of two of the largest U.S. Government agencies: the Department of Health and Human Services (HHS) and the Department of Homeland Security (DHS), where she honed her passion for managing programs with a strong focus on how to define programmatic and mission success. Prior to her role at NASA Headquarters, Kathy demonstrated her dynamic systems approach, leading diverse public and private organizations in the development of business partnerships.

Kathy is skilled in developing relationships as well as implementing change; she can communicate clear and concise messages and build cohesive and collaborative teams that deliver world-class products to the customer, the public, and stakeholders. She has broad expertise in the strategic development of legislative advocacy products and has led program and policy integration teams for large-scale scientific and engineering programs.

Outside of work, Kathy has led her fraternity's local alumnae group, served for over two decades as an officer or board member for one of America's premier aerospace organizations of space professionals dedicated to advancing all space activities, and become a requested mentor with the Severn Leadership Group (SLG). Kathy is an active member of her faith community, and she loves singing in choirs, riding bikes, gardening, and sailing on the Chesapeake Bay with her friends.

Connect with Kathy:

Facebook: https://www.facebook.com/kathy.nado.9

LinkedIn: https://www.linkedin.com/in/kathynado/

CHAPTER FOUR

THE RESTORATIVE POWER OF UNCONDITIONAL TRUST

HOW MENTORS HELP NAVIGATE TRYING TIMES

Colin Pascal

MY STORY

An exceptional mentor can help a person regain faith in themselves after everything else falls apart. In January 2024, as a lieutenant colonel in the Army, I learned that lesson after being relieved from battalion command. It was devastating.

Being relieved in the military is like being fired as a civilian, and there's little hope of ever professionally recovering. I spent 52 months deployed to Iraq and Afghanistan, earned elite qualifications in my field, was a commander three times, and held some of the most sensitive positions in the Defense Intelligence Enterprise. Until the day I was relieved, I expected to finish my command and be promoted to colonel and then serve in uniform for another ten years. This was the first time I faced rejection from an institution I loved.

Except for losing my sister, who died in her 20s while I was overseas in Iraq, watching my career end was the hardest thing I've ever faced. In a moment, I went from someone with an exceptional record and a bright future to a person who would struggle to ever be taken seriously again as a military officer.

Few things mattered more to me than the Army. Nothing gave me as much satisfaction as leading soldiers on missions that mattered. Realizing I would never have that chance again was shocking, especially since the Army had been my only adult job and was foundational to who I believed I was. Being relieved left me unsettled, fearful, and lost.

My memories of that time have faded, and the emotions have turned from sharp to dull. However, I'm grateful to still remember some things clearly, as the experience has now become an important part of who I've become. First were the sleepless nights and worry. *My best days are behind me, and my future is unsatisfying and small.* I recall the family, friends, and former colleagues whose support sustained me, as well as a recently retired Air Force brigadier general named John Teichert. He was the first person I viewed as a mentor, and he used that unique position in my life to help navigate a particularly difficult time. His steady support was the foundation on which I rebuilt my future, and he helped me rediscover a sense of purpose and self-worth.

I knew General Teichert from our time together in Baghdad, when he was the Senior Defense Official and Military Attaché, and I was the Chief of Human Intelligence and Counterintelligence for Operation Inherent Resolve. We were based at the U.S. Embassy and got to know each other because the embassy had been nearly evacuated after militia groups repeatedly targeted the compound with rockets. General Teichert and I were two of the relatively few who remained.

"Call me John," he said when both of us retired. But old habits die hard, and I couldn't bring myself to use his first name. Calling him "sir" was too formal in civilian clothes, so I settled on the call sign he earned as an Air Force pilot. "John won't work for me, but I think I can call you Dragon." Since that's the way I address him, it's what I'll call him here.

It's important to understand who Dragon is before exploring what he did for me as a mentor. I've never met a deeper thinker or more selfless leader. He was the first and only general officer I ever met who ended conversations by asking, "How can I help?" and his concern for people was always clear. I never worked for Dragon directly, so it wasn't his job to take care of me in Baghdad, but he did anyway and made me feel like a member of his team.

Dragon invited me to the Friday socials he hosted for senior officers and allowed me to sneak in as a lieutenant colonel even though others in attendance were colonels. Those Friday gatherings gave me a professional network and a sense of camaraderie, even though my chain of command and the people I led were far away and scattered across bases in Iraq, Syria, and Kuwait. The relationships Dragon facilitated for me by including me in those events helped me accomplish things that wouldn't have been possible if I were just a lieutenant colonel navigating the embassy on my own. When I spoke, people listened. Not because they knew me, but because they knew and respected Dragon and could tell that he trusted me enough to consider my opinion.

We stayed in touch after we returned from Baghdad. This was new for me since I had never prioritized maintaining professional relationships, even with senior officers who might help my career. But I had watched Dragon argue hard and unpopular points at interagency meetings, produce insightful reports for policy makers, inspire the best in his team, and build relationships with Iraqi leaders that many of us thought were impossible. He was willing to take thoughtful risks when most leaders had become completely risk averse. He was the type of leader I respected but rarely found, and I looked up to him, so I tried to stay in contact and was grateful that he reciprocated.

Dragon took up a new post as Assistant Deputy Undersecretary of the Air Force for International Affairs, and I was given command of a military intelligence battalion, the most sought-after achievement for an Army lieutenant colonel and a validation of nearly two decades of hard work. Dragon attended my change of command ceremony, his Air Force flight suit and general's star adding a bit of interest to the affair. I expected to invite him to a second ceremony two years later—the one where I relinquished command, but I never made it that far. After 18 months, I was relieved of command.

I'll always regret that I wasn't able to connect with and inspire the group of people who complained about my leadership, nor maintain the trust and confidence of my immediate supervisor. Two surveys found that support for my leadership was above 80%, and many more people wrote statements supporting me than ever wrote statements against. Despite how it ended, I'm proud of what I accomplished.

The battalion I led has undergone significant reorganization and refocusing, and I initiated the modernization process with the goal of enhancing the unit's impact. I look back on the experience with humility and gratitude for the extraordinary people who made our successes possible. But those healthy emotions weren't a foregone conclusion. It was Dragon's mentorship during one of the hardest times of my life that was most responsible for the peaceful and productive place I eventually found at the end of my Army career.

I was relieved at the end of January, and the next two months were the most challenging and darkest time. I was grateful my children weren't old enough to understand what had happened, and fearful I would never again find a way to make them proud. I used to take long drives because I wasn't sure what else to do. I couldn't stand being home while the world continued to move forward and I stood still. I might have fallen off the cliff into depression, but four things pulled me through.

First, my family, whose love was unconditional, especially my wife and two young children; second, my faith, knowing the Holy Spirit was with me even in those darkest days; third, my relationships, as dozens of people expressed support and solidarity; fourth, the unconditional trust Dragon placed in me, which reminded me I was a good and productive person.

Nobody but a mentor could have offered the type of support Dragon provided because mentors occupy such a unique place in people's lives. Because they tend to be older and farther along in their careers, and because their support isn't required by family ties, the validation they offer feels earned and freely given. *If he thinks I'm a good person and a good officer, then I must be, because I trust his judgement completely.* That thought kept me from losing myself, and if Dragon believed in me, I knew I should, too.

THE STRATEGY

As I reflected on those early months as my Army career ended, I realized Dragon did several very specific things that helped me move forward. First, he trusted me unconditionally. Second, he created a sense of normalcy. Third, he gave me a mission. These three steps were critical to my recovery and can be replicated by mentors who find themselves helping people through challenging times.

UNCONDITIONAL TRUST

When I asked Dragon for a character reference as part of the fight to save my career, he agreed to give it without asking why I needed it. I remember trying to explain the situation to him but stumbling because I didn't have the words yet to describe what was happening. Somewhere in the middle of my muddled explanation, he interrupted me politely but with force and said something I'll never forget.

"Colin, you can tell me about it if you want to, but I'm happy to write you a letter even if you don't. I know who you are." This was the moment, and those were the words, when my emotional decline stopped and the first feelings of steadiness returned.

By not asking me for an explanation, Dragon demonstrated the immense power of a mentor's unconditional trust, washing away my fear that the people I respected most would no longer respect me.

This type of unconditional trust is difficult to give. Had Dragon asked for the details, even if he ended up writing the letter after fully understanding the situation, my reaction to his support would have been far less pronounced. It's natural for mentors to want an explanation before offering their support, and I was prepared to share every detail. But that would have been exhausting at a time when I was already tired, and it would have felt like having to re-earn his trust. That would have been one more reminder of the many things I had lost. But Dragon never asked, and that unconditional trust did more to restore me than anything else he could have done.

NORMALCY

During the most abnormal period of my life, Dragon acted normally. It was common in the early months for people to feel sorry for me or to express anger over what had happened. These reactions are understandable but aren't helpful. What I needed was the peace that comes from normalcy— normalcy created by a continuation of things as they existed before. In the months following my relief, Dragon communicated with me the same way he always had, which reassured me that not everything in my life had changed and some very important things would endure. After he wrote his letter of support, almost none of our interactions were about what happened at the end of my career. And that was exactly what I needed: normal conversation about normal things that helped turn an abnormal time into something more familiar.

MISSION

Soon after he retired from the Air Force, Dragon sought the Republican Party's nomination for U.S. Senate in my adopted home state of Maryland. I've been a registered Democrat my entire adult life and there are places in policy where Dragon and I might disagree. But those differences pale in comparison to the things we hold in common: Reverence for the Constitution, belief in the goodness of America, deep faith in God, and an unshakable optimism for the future.

I was still on active duty during Dragon's campaign and couldn't participate as fully as I would have liked, but I corresponded with him frequently and shared my thoughts and encouragement. He always wrote back thoughtfully, which was amazing, given the complexity of his schedule at the time. That correspondence gave me my first sense of a new purpose and a new mission as I took a few tentative steps into the world of politics and contributed in a small way to a campaign that mattered.

That sense of mission was a gift that only a mentor could have provided. Lots of people could suggest ways to fill my time, but only someone of Dragon's stature in my life could make our simple correspondence feel like a mission. It helped that he was involved in such a big endeavor, but even if he hadn't been running for U.S. Senate, he could have given me the same sense of purpose by including me in whatever he happened to be engaged with at the time.

In February 2024, Maryland's former Governor Larry Hogan unexpectedly entered the Senate race, and Dragon did the honorable thing by ending his campaign to support the candidate who was best placed to win. He took up a post as Chair of the Veterans for Hogan Coalition, and as I approached retirement from active duty, he invited me to join. I ended up attending several campaign events and publishing three op-eds and two letters explaining my support for Hogan in *The Baltimore Sun, The Baltimore Banner,* and *The Washington Post.* I also gave two short television interviews on local channels, and one that aired nationally on *PBS Newshour.*

Governor Hogan was gracious and even more decent in person than the positive image he portrays in the media. I feel fortunate that I got to know him a bit and that my six-year-old daughter, Claire, had a front-row seat to his positive style of campaigning. Hogan's kindness and dignity were the perfect introduction for Claire to the beauty of American democracy.

The little bit of work I did for Hogan's campaign, and the writing on politics and international affairs I've continued to publish, are what allowed me to turn the last hard corner in my transition to a new purpose after the Army. But all of that was only possible because Dragon trusted me, included me, and treated me normally, as if nothing bad had happened. He never minimized my loss or my emotions, but he never made sorrow or looking backwards the central part of our interactions.

He also never uttered a single negative word about the people who hurt me, and he never showed the slightest bit of cynicism or anger toward a system that both of us believed had failed. It's not in my nature to dwell on the negative, but like any person, I might have let anger and resentment get the best of me, but for the dignified and respectful way that Dragon spoke about everyone involved.

Dragon never commiserated in my few moments of negativity, and he showed how important it is for mentors to guard against that temptation as they help people through hard times. One of the most important things a mentor can do, as Dragon did, is set an example of civility, compassion, and understanding, especially toward the people who may have been unfair, misinformed, or wrong.

Dragon knew that assigning blame is often difficult and nearly always unproductive, especially in the months following a tragedy. His own aversion to blaming people, and the equal respect he showed toward me and toward the people whose decisions had hurt me, helped me avoid the common trap of placing blame. Had he suggested in any way that blaming others was the right thing to do, in that moment of weakness, I might have been eager to follow. Instead, he led me away from that path and saved me from the unhappy and unproductive fate that blaming others always brings.

My friends and family, especially my wife, deserve enormous credit for their patience and love as I sought new meaning in my life after my Army career ended. They were part of a bridge that led from one of the hardest times to one of the happiest times in my life. So much good has come since I left the Army: my deep involvement with St. Anne's Episcopal Church, volunteering as a mentor with Severn Leadership Group; collecting diapers for families in need with Walk the Walk Foundation; serving as a volunteer counselor at a camp for kids from lower-income households, corresponding with a former governor; writing commentaries for respected regional and national publications; and going back to graduate school at American University in Washington, D.C. Dragon was the person most responsible for making those good things possible, and those are the things that taken together saved me. His actions in those early days not only steadied me, but they also inspired me to find new meaning as only a mentor could. By showing me unconditional trust, creating a sense of normalcy, and giving me a mission, Dragon changed my life.

Colin Pascal is a retired Army lieutenant colonel who spent most of his 20-year military career filling strategic intelligence assignments. He commanded the U.S. Army Special Investigations Detachment, responsible for the Army's most sensitive counterintelligence and counterterrorism investigations, Alpha Company/201st Military Intelligence Battalion, a strategic interrogation unit he led while deployed to Afghanistan, and the Operations Support Battalion, responsible for safeguarding the Army's most highly classified secrets. He served as Assistant Army Attaché at the U.S. Embassy in Baghdad and as Chief of Counterintelligence and Human Intelligence for Operation INHERENT RESOLVE in Iraq and Syria.

Colin is a graduate of the Advanced Foreign Counterintelligence Operations Course, the National Security Investigations Course, the Counterintelligence Surveillance Course, the Defense Strategic Debriefing Course, the U.S. Army Counterintelligence Special Agent Course, the Joint Military Attaché Course, and other Army, Joint and Interagency intelligence courses. He deployed four times to Iraq and once to Afghanistan and holds a bachelor's degree in history from St. Bonaventure University, as well as a Master of Military Art and Science from the U.S. Army Command and General Staff College. He is pursuing a Master of Public Administration at American University in Washington, D.C. He lives in Annapolis, Maryland, with his wife Caroline, daughter Claire, and son Casey.

Connect with Colin:

Email: colinjpascal@outlook.com

LinkedIn: www.linkedin.com/in/colin-pascal-09b166324

PART: 2

UNDERSTANDING YOURSELF AS A MENTOR

CHAPTER FIVE

YOUR "WHY" MATTERS

FUELING RESILIENCE
THROUGH MOTIVATION

Rob Shepherd

When people ask me how I motivate my people,
my answer is that I don't. I don't try to push or pull people.
Instead, I try to inspire people and help them find their own motivations.

~ John Maxwell

MY STORY

Why does this have to be so hard?

Branson, Missouri, is a wonderful resort town with beautiful lakes, world-class music venues, and endless wares from local artisans. Aside from the amusement park, however, it's not a great destination for a high school senior trip.

My classmate shook me to consciousness just after midnight to hand me the telephone. "Hello?"

"Congratulations, son. You're going to the Naval Academy." My dad's voice betrayed his attempt to remain emotionless.

"That's great. Good night, Dad." I stretched to put the receiver back on the telephone, rolled over, and fell fast asleep.

When I woke up, I had to confirm the conversation with my friends. Sure enough, they verified the details. Though I dreamed of being an Air Force pilot, I knew that I'd have a more difficult path now. *Why?*

My family rallied around me, helping to craft a path from the Naval Academy into the Air Force. *Where is Annapolis? I can't even swim. How am I going to survive the next four years?*

Although none of my early mentors used the phrase, I have come to realize that this trial—and those to come—were developing in me the ability to bounce back, or resilience. I would need every bit of it as I graduated from Annapolis, received my commission in the Air Force, and headed to Undergraduate Pilot Training in Texas.

After proving myself as a first-assignment instructor pilot day after day, I expected to be selected for a coveted, open evaluator position.

The boss must remember how well I managed his recent checkout in the squadron. Now it's time for my reward.

The call never came. One of my closest friends got the position. My heart sank.

Colonel Robinson, don't you remember how well I took care of you? How could you have abandoned me? I made an appointment to see him to resolve this whole matter.

"That job was never yours, Rob." Colonel Robinson's words echoed in my mind, but they didn't make sense. "I've long planned another position for you."

How could I have been so impetuous? He has my best interests in mind, and I'm in here whining like a baby at nap time. Am I being resilient?

After nearly five years as a T-37 instructor, I could see my next assignment on the horizon. I did everything asked of me during that tour, garnering accolades and hopefully changing the lives of some new pilots for the better.

"None of you are getting fighter assignments," the wing commander explained. The Gulf War had just ended, and the number of fighter squadrons declined.

My jaw dropped.

What?! After all I've done? I guess it's time for plan B—what's the next best thing?

The answer lay just ahead: I would be flying the C-5 in California. As I adjusted to my new assignment, a voice of reason appeared in the form of my flight commander. Major George Worley taught me much I needed to know, taking me from the still-agitated wannabe fighter pilot to a budding leader among my peers. He helped me understand the importance of the global airlift mission in the early 1990s and refocused my attention on one of the Air Force's core values: service before self.

That's what I've been missing this whole time. I've been so mindful of my desires that I've missed the bigger picture. Perhaps I've been placed here for a reason.

God orchestrated all these events behind the scenes, and I was beginning to connect the dots. I wouldn't have met the love of my life at the Army-Navy game if I had gone to the Air Force Academy. Although my hoped-for evaluator role got more flying time, I was much better suited to the position I eventually occupied. And one of my early Air Force advisors, who flew the F-15, told me he would have probably made the Air Force a career if he'd been a C-5 pilot instead.

Resilience brought me through these setbacks, but there was something still deeper at work here. God wanted me to discover His plan for my life.

I became a senior fellow with the Severn Leadership Group (SLG) several years later, which led to a key inflection point. The timing seemed providential. I recently retired from the Air Force and had no ready outlet for my years of leadership training. *What perfect timing! I can share all my wisdom with these Fellows.* Pride lurked at my door.

Author and entrepreneur Simon Sinek joined our group for a conversation in the living room of one of SLG's founders. Sinek's first book, *Start with WHY,* captivated my mind, and I was eager to engage with him about his time at Southwest Airlines while researching for his book. He encouraged me to connect with his team to help discover my reason for being, my "WHY." (Simon uses all capitals throughout his book.)

My "why" revealed itself to me over several hours of conversation with a friend: "To engage people so that relationships bear fruit through a sense of worth, community, and personal growth." That was surprising because I didn't think I liked people. I love God's sense of humor!

Sinek notes in *Start with WHY,* "When I say WHY, I don't mean to make money—that's a result. By WHY, I mean what is your purpose, cause, or belief? WHY does your company exist? WHY do you get out of bed every morning? And WHY should anyone care?" (Sinek, 2011). I did exactly what the writer of Proverbs discouraged by "lean[ing] on [my] own understanding" (Proverbs 3:5 ESV) rather than ordering my thoughts according to God's revealed plan.

Armed with a clarified sense of purpose, I began to look at many of my choices and see a larger picture. My military career ended, but I still flew professionally and sought advancement. *Why?* I looked for ways to serve in my church, like singing in an Easter cantata. *Why?* The SLG Fellows Program has a mentorship dimension, so I volunteered my time in that capacity.

Why? These activities are helping me engage people in fruit-bearing relationships. Maybe knowing and embracing my why will make my road straight and level.

Charlie (not his real name) was an SLG Fellow and member of my church. Upon our first meeting, we connected famously. Charlie loved to ski; I grew up in Denver, skiing from the age of two. I was a disciple-maker; he was growing in his faith and eager to serve the Lord.

Our relationship flourished until we disagreed on a doctrinal point about how Jesus might have led. *I've been through more than this before. This is just a pothole on our relational freeway, and my resilience will smooth it over.*

We worked on the issue, but Charlie couldn't overcome his apprehension about my point of view, effectively ending our mentor/protégé relationship.

What happened? I'm following my why, and it's not working. Or maybe I didn't consider what Charlie wanted from our time together.

Taking a few moments early in our relationship to clarify his goals may have better prepared me for the conversation and could have preempted the conflict. My own understanding was clear, but failure to see things from Charlie's perspective made me inflexible. When trouble arrived, I broke instead of bending.

I have also been a part of the C.S. Lewis Institute in Annapolis since 2012, serving as a Fellow and mentor. Jim Phillips, the founding City Director, and I were having dinner one evening with our wives when he asked me the classic question: "What do you want to be when you grow up?" I held him in the very highest regard but still answered somewhat flippantly: "I want to be you." *You're so clever!*

Months later, as I described my plan to begin a seminary program, Jim reminded me of that conversation. "Let me offer an alternative plan," he said after listening carefully. "I feel called to get my PhD, and I can't do this (serve as the City Director) at the same time." *I feel like my life is about to undergo a significant change.* My pulse quickened. "Can I get back to you?" I followed the Spirit's leading and stepped into the breach.

Our relationship changed over the following months as Jim sought to understand my willingness to take on the director's responsibilities. He gave me clear and relevant guidance because he discovered my why.

I now serve as a Standards Check Airman with Southwest Airlines, primarily charged with mentoring the rest of our Check Airmen. *I have finally found the object of my why! I know why these pilots are serving as evaluators, and I'm helping a worthy community grow personally and professionally.*

Maybe knowing my purpose could have straightened my path up to this point, but at least I developed a mature resilience upon which I can rely.

THE STRATEGY

Mentoring relationships can help both partners cultivate resilience and benefit from it when things get tough. Let's look at ways we can create the right environment for this to happen.

KNOW YOUR WHY

All the information-gathering questions (who, what, when, where, how, and why) will help guide the search for a mentor or protégé, but your reason for forming such a relationship will have a crucial impact on the quality of your affiliation.

Unlike Sinek, I'm not suggesting you consider your overarching why. Rather, you should uncover your reasons for serving as someone's mentor.

Dr. Jim Phillips saw a potential successor for his role as CSLI Annapolis City Director, which is a form of corporate mentorship with a pragmatic aspect. But his intentions were far from transactional, because "the Scriptures command us to disciple and teach others" (personal communication, May 30, 2025).

Discovering your mentoring why can be a straightforward process:

1. Consider why you've looked for mentors in the past. Perhaps you were climbing the corporate ladder and recognized the need for insights about your aspirational position you couldn't obtain without inside help. A mentor within your agency might have been considering succession planning. You may be able to repay that gesture in kind and have a desire to do so now.

2. Ask your protégé why he selected you, or ask yourself why you chose him. The selection process can be awkward—who chooses who and to what end? A formal mentoring program can place two people together for a particular purpose, while more informal relationships might develop in response to the needs of one or the other partner. The format might drive the behaviors within the relationship, guiding your purpose for engaging with the other.

HELP YOUR PROTÉGÉS KNOW WHY

While it's important to understand your reasons for serving as a mentor, it's only one factor. Remember my mentoring failure with Charlie? I believe the root cause was misaligned expectations because I didn't explore why he sought out a mentor. I could have built more trust—critical to a resilient relationship—by better proving my concern for his needs.

Here are some foundational steps to ensure you make the right connection with your protégés from the outset:

1. Make the protégé the center of attention. You should learn as much as you can about her as soon as possible. This requires active listening and patience. Resist the desire to share too much about yourself—there will be plenty of time for that later.

2. Ask thought-provoking questions to draw out the other party. One of the most common looks at legacy, such as "What would your obituary say?" You could also use more near-term ones, like "What problems would you love to solve?" You can discern emotional issues as well by asking about when your protégé feels fulfilled and considering how that might stimulate other behavior.

   Dr. Phillips used this to help me work through a period of discouragement as City Director, pointing out that I lit up when describing a creative project I undertook. I understood my pessimism was misplaced because it didn't affect my underlying reasons for serving the Institute.

3. Focus on empathy. Think of this as "perspective taking," involving not just a cognitive understanding of your protégé, but also engaging in an affective connection. You want to appreciate his environment and desires.

4. Guide her toward clarity of expectations. Remember, you are trying to help your protégé discover her motivations rather than providing a checklist for success. She should anticipate more questions than answers.

CHALLENGE ASSUMPTIONS

We make assumptions about how we and others see the world in order to manage the thousands of decisions we must make every day. However, as Henry Winkler said, "Assumptions are the termites of relationships" (Winkler, 2025). Even if the assumptions later prove to be correct, failure to examine them may leave our blind spots intact, leading us to unwisely trust our intuition and create a tenuous connection with our protégés.

This ties in with your protégé's goals within the relationship. If he isn't clear about the reasons for getting together, you may both wander into the wilderness. For instance, suppose you are trained as a counselor and your protégé is struggling to maintain emotional stability at work. You may sense an underlying mental concern and offer a therapeutic solution, while he is simply dealing with a difficult boss and seeking practical advice. Some open dialogue could avert this confusion.

1. Ask direct questions. Mentoring is not for the timid, and shared expectations may not readily appear. When my children were young, they would sometimes say, "Dad, are you hungry?" as we passed by one of our favorite restaurants. My wife and I addressed this coy comment, asking them to simply tell us what they wanted. Look for implicit expectations that either of you might have and bring them into the light by openly addressing them. This can kill Winkler's destructive termites.

2. Provide frequent check-in opportunities, asking questions such as, "What are we missing in our conversation?" or "Is this what you meant?" This can pave the way for a deeper exploration of unspoken beliefs before they become deeply held expectations.

3. Listen. I can struggle with quietly listening after asking a thought-provoking question, which sometimes limits my ability to integrate the answer into the conversation. Listen for both content and emotion to help you chart the path forward.

4. Withhold judgment. Whether or not your assumptions are correct isn't really the issue, so don't focus on their accuracy. Rather, make sure you understand their implications. Using our example of a protégé's difficult boss, your assessment of your partner's need for therapy may be valid but unrecognized on his part. Deal with his expectations first, and then perhaps the window will open for further conversation about your perception of his additional needs.

REMEMBER YOUR WHY—BOTH OF YOU!

Revisiting your reasons for mentoring—and asking the same of your protégé—can breathe life into your relationship.

1. Review your progress. "Are we heading in the right direction?" This powerful question is open-ended enough to give the protégé much latitude in describing the situation and signal your willingness to modify your approach.

2. Hold your plans loosely and don't be afraid to change direction. We bring some agenda into our interactions with others, even when we're trying to be other-centered. Add a healthy dose of humility and keep those three wonderful words close at hand—"I was wrong"—to demonstrate your ability to follow your protégé's lead in the relationship.

3. Allow for an organic termination. A keen understanding of why—for both of you—can help set the scope of the relationship. Your protégé may have made other professional contacts because of your guidance, in which case "the time and energy of both parties is rightly transferred to their new working relationships" (Ensher and Murphy, 2005).

REFINE YOUR WHY

I grow along with my protégés, even when the going gets tough, but I'm still not the expert that I envision in my mind's eye. Stephen Covey's seventh habit, "Sharpen the saw," (Covey, 1989) gives us some guidance to move closer to mastery. We must take time to refine our motivations—our why—to be as resilient as possible for those who seek us out.

To summarize:

1. Know why you're a mentor

2. Find out what your protégé needs

3. Maintain a shared mental model

4. Keep why at the forefront of the relationship

You can use these practices before you begin to mentor, while you're actively engaged in a mentoring relationship, and while reflecting on past experiences to boost your readiness for the next encounter. The most important thing to do is to use them. Your why won't protect you from setbacks, but it will carry you through them as a mentor worth emulating.

References

Covey, Stephen R. 1989. *The Seven Habits of Highly Effective People: Restoring the Character Ethic.* Simon & Schuster.

Ensher, Ellen A. and Susan E. Murphy. 2005. *Power Mentoring: How Successful Mentors and Protégés Get the Most Out of Their Relationships.* San Francisco, California: Jossey-Bass.

Henry Winkler Quotes. BrainyQuote.com, BrainyMedia Inc., 2025. https://www.brainyquote.com/quotes/henry_winkler_320340, accessed May 30, 2025.

Sinek, S., 2011. *Start with Why: How Great Leaders Inspire Everyone to Take Action,* London: Penguin Books Ltd.

Rob Shepherd is a Senior Fellow with the Severn Leadership Group, an Annapolis-based group that seeks to inspire lives of selfless courage and service to others. He's also a Baltimore-based Captain for Southwest Airlines, having retired from the Air Force after 25 years flying mostly airlift aircraft and serving in three command positions.

Rob holds degrees in Computer Science from the U.S. Naval Academy (B.S.) and the University of Idaho (M.S.). He completed the C.S. Lewis Insitute Fellows Program, an intensive, community-oriented Christian discipleship program, has served as a mentor for the Fellows Program, and leads the Institute in Annapolis as City Director.

When he's not traveling, Rob enjoys cruising the Chesapeake Bay with his wife on their Ranger Tug *Kairos*, reading, and running. He and Mary Beth have two grown children and two granddaughters, who are the apples of his eye.

Connect with Rob:

Website: https://www.cslewisinstitute.org/annapolis/

LinkedIn: https://www.linkedin.com/in/rob-shepherd-8b1189/

Email: r.shepherd@cslewisinstitute.org

CHAPTER SIX

KNOWING YOURSELF, GROWING OTHERS

USING EQ TO CULTIVATE SELF-AWARENESS

Kristen Dombrowski, CPCC, PCC

MY STORY

Surely, I was more mature than this!

I thought I was pretty developed: well-read, self-aware, decades into personal growth.

So, when I scored surprisingly low on a maturity assessment, it was a gut-punch!

Many years ago, I came across the vertical development theory. Unlike most self-development approaches that focus on how you fill your cup, this one asks: *What if you could expand the cup?* I was hooked! I took the assessment, excited to see where I stood in my adult development journey.

But then, disappointment.

Despite my years of study, training, development, coaching, and life experience, I scored lower than I imagined.

Fueled by determination—and, let's be honest, ego—I hired a coach-mentor, Lucille Greeff.

Until this point in my life, growth was invigorating. I raced toward it like a kid on a bike flying through summer sprinklers—full speed, no helmet, no fear of falling. Learning and doing new things was my playground. I showed up to my first session with Lucille, pen in hand, new, crisp notebook, eager to ascend to the next stage of maturity.

And then, something in me shifted.

As Lucille began to describe what that next stage required, I slowed down. I hit the brakes on my bike. Because to grow, I'd have to let go of everything I thought was a recipe for success: my hard-won systems, my beliefs, and several parts of my identity.

Somewhere deep inside, a hard truth started to surface, but not fully. I heard myself say to her unexpectedly, with tears: "I want to go on this journey, but I don't want to touch my religion or my marriage."

I hadn't realized yet how tightly I'd been holding onto those areas of my life. How fragile they were. Because I wasn't ready to look at them, they were my no-go zone and definitely off-limits.

Many coaches or mentors would have jumped in with, "Well, that's exactly where you need to go!" But not Lucille. She simply said, "Okay." And then she gently offered an invitation—resources I could explore *if and when* I was ready, but she let it go.

That moment built trust not just in her, but within me again. I didn't feel pushed; I felt seen. So, I picked up speed on my bike again, feeling safe and supported to continue the ride. And wouldn't you know—within six months, I began questioning my religion. Within a few years, my marriage ended.

Looking back, it's clear: I held those parts of my life together with Scotch tape, idealization, and a prayer.

But Lucille never forced me to face anything. She simply held up a mirror and waited. When I was ready to look—really look—at the parts of me I didn't want to see and kept hidden, she was there as she always was. With a growing strength, she helped me develop my map and shape my journey of growth. I found myself riding down roads I'd never explored before. This ride felt different, less like a child trying to go as fast as they can, but one with more purpose and intention. This ride felt stronger, more grounded—even mature, dare I say.

I don't need to take another maturity assessment to know how far I've come. I'm dismantling the very structures I thought defined me (some by choice and some not). I also stepped into the painful, humbling side of real growth and development, as well as the beautiful side of healing. Not the shiny kind, but the soul-deep, scar-lined kind.

Over the years, I've come to deeply respect Lucille's holistic way of mentoring: not as a fixer, not as a pusher, but as a mirror and a map. She met me exactly where I was. She walked beside me, not ahead of me. She offered invitations and what she called "heat experiences," not challenges. And when I was ready, I walked through doors that I once locked shut.

I offer my personal story and the powerful transformations possible for those who want to become holistic, heart-centered mentors. It's also a letter of love and gratitude to one of the most remarkable humans I've ever had the honor to be mentored by.

THE STRATEGY

Mirror and Map
A Self-Perception Tool for Holistic Mentors

Most of us think of ourselves as thinking creatures who feel, but we are actually feeling creatures who think.

~ Dr. Jill Bolte Taylor

WHY THIS MATTERS

Life happens constantly, and all day long, we experience feelings in response to what unfolds around us. Those feelings lead to thoughts, and those thoughts become stories—ways to explain our world and our place in it. This process is swift and mostly unconscious, drawing on past experiences and beliefs to cultivate the stories we tell ourselves.

Without slowing the process and creating some intentional self-reflection, we climb the "Ladder of Inference" (Argyris, *Harvard Business Review*), jumping to conclusions we feel are true about people and situations but are often rooted in bias, fear, or outdated/limited beliefs.

Emotional Intelligence (EQ) helps us slow down those processes to make them conscious and visible to ourselves. EQ is a tool that can help you see how much access you have to different emotional and social functioning behaviors that contribute to your overall well-being and relationships with others. Thus, emotional intelligence becomes essential, especially in mentoring roles.

If you're a mentor, your presence matters. And if you want to support someone else's growth, your ability to reflect, regulate, and choose wisely in your emotional inner landscape is key.

As we create balance in our access to EQ elements, we create a space and a practice for clarity, growth, openness, and curiosity. Consequently, we create options rather than conclusions to our stories. This is essential for mentors: not to direct, fix, or be triggered, but to hold space to reflect (with a mirror) and walk beside your mentee on their journey (on their map).

THE MIRROR AND MAP FRAMEWORK

The Mirror: Self-Awareness

The mirror represents your capacity for self-awareness. It reflects what you already know, what you don't know, what you admire about yourself, and what you want to keep hidden. It invites you to observe without judgment. It represents the EQ elements, both emotional self-awareness and self-regard: seeing yourself clearly and with acceptance, including your light and shadow.

The mirror shows:

- The emotions you're feeling.
- The thoughts that follow those emotions.
- The physical signals your body gives.
- The deeper virtues, values, and needs those feelings are pointing toward.

The mirror helps you answer the question: *What is true in me right now?*

The Map: Journey

The map is where your self-reflection becomes intentional action and movement. With a clearer sense of self, you can choose where you want to go and who you want to become by going to the places that matter most. It represents the EQ elements self-actualization and self-regard again: setting direction based on values, needs, and inner capability.

- What direction aligns with your core values?
- What inner terrain do you want to explore or develop?
- What kind of mentor—and human—do you want to be?

The map is your values in action, which are your virtues—values lived out in practicality. It's how you take the self-awareness from the mirror and apply it to your goals, habits, relationships, and personal growth.

The map helps you ask: *Where am I going, and why?*

The Self-Perception Composite of EQ-i 2.0: The Inner Game

The three elements in this composite build the foundation for self-leadership. They're inward facing but deeply impact how you relate to others. For mentors, this triad creates the emotional resilience and clarity needed to support others.

- **Emotional Self-Awareness:** Am I aware of what I'm feeling and why?
- **Self-Regard:** Do I like and accept who I am, as I am?
- **Self-Actualization:** Am I pursuing what matters most to me with purpose and vitality?

TWO-PART STRATEGY: MIRROR & MAP WITH EQ

Step 1. The Mirror: Starting with Emotional Self-Awareness

Before you can lead, support, or guide others, you must turn inward. Emotional self-awareness is not just about knowing you feel something— it's knowing what you feel, why you feel it, and what it might be telling you. Self-regard complements this by helping you face that awareness with acceptance and self-compassion.

Short Practice (10–14 Days)

Create a daily observational practice of emotional tracking:

Set Daily Checkpoints:

- Choose three to five consistent times per day (e.g., nine a.m., noon, four p.m., eight p.m.).
- Use an emotions wheel or list to create some language for yourself about your emotions.
- Spend three to five minutes reflecting using a journal, voice memo, or app.

Record:

- What emotion(s) am I feeling? (Maybe more than one is present for you.)
- What thoughts are connected to these feelings? (Be honest with yourself!)
- What's happening in my body (clenched jaw, hot neck, shaky legs, sick stomach)?
- What's happening around me (people, place, conversations, sounds, etc.)?

Self-Reflection (After Ten to 14 Days):

- Are there patterns or themes emerging?
- What values, needs, or motivations are under the surface?
- What triggers seem to be consistent?
- What seems to be important to me?

Longer-Term Practices:

- **Assessments:** Take the EQ-i 2.0 to understand your emotional and social functioning across all composites. Take a values assessment to clarify what drives and motivates you.

- **Mentor/Coach:** Explore your self-perception, patterns, blind spots, and emotional responses to see more of the evidence and expand some of your beliefs.

- **Reflection Tools:** Use weekly journaling prompts or group dialogue to continue the practice of staying present to your emotional state.

Step 2. The Map: Using Self-Regard and Self-Actualization to Move Forward

Once you've gathered insight from your mirror practice, begin using that insight to navigate growth. Self-regard is essential here again—it gives you the courage to acknowledge both your strengths and your shadows. Self-actualization then becomes the energy behind setting goals and moving toward a life of alignment.

Self-Regard: Accepting All Parts of You

Self-regard is not about being arrogant or having inflated self-esteem. It's the ability to see all of yourself and still affirm your worth.

Reflective Prompts:

- How much do I like myself right now (one to ten, with ten being "I like all parts of me!")?

- What strengths, values, or traits make that number possible?

  o Not why I did not give myself a ten, but what do I like enough about myself to give myself the number I did?

- What number would feel healthy and right—not perfect?

- What compassionate step or shift can I take toward that?

- What would one small (or big) step toward that version of me look like?

Embracing all of yourself—especially the less polished or more reactive parts—enables deeper integration and emotional maturity. You stop overidentifying with your wounds or compensating with overused strengths. You become whole.

Possible Map Ideas

- Daily gratitude journal with prompts.
- Write three positive affirmations in the morning and consider them in the evening.
- When you make mistakes, have compassion like you would for a child, someone you love, or a pet.
- Journaling, meditation, praying, and breathwork. These are not one-size-fits-all; there are many different modalities for each, so find the one that works for you.

Self-Actualization: Living on Purpose

Self-actualization is your capacity to strive, to dream, to live in alignment with what gives you fuel for forward motion.

Reflective Prompts:

- **Past:** What's one meaningful success and one hard lesson from the last two years?
- **Present:** How aligned are my current actions with my deepest beliefs?
- **Future:** What do I want to do more of, less of, or differently?
  - Who do I need to be to sustain that future?
  - What support, mindset, or habit do I need to cultivate?

- **Additional Considerations:**
  - What strengths do I want to lean into more?
  - What beliefs might I need to challenge?
  - What boundaries or habits will support my growth?

Possible Map Ideas

- Set some *SMART* goals, both long-term and short-term, around self, lifestyle, and career.

- Identify strengths and challenge yourself to use your strengths in a new and different way each day for two weeks.

- Identify your stretch zone with the goals, which is between your comfort zone and the panic zone. This is where you're motivated and energized.

- Consistent self-reflection of prompts and goals to consider progress made/not made, and next steps, even if the decision is not going forward with the goal anymore. Sometimes with action comes clarity of a new, more important goal!

THE MENTOR'S ROLE: HOLDING MIRROR AND MAP

Having a practice of doing your inner work:

- Keeps your emotional landscape clear.

- Helps you respond—not react—to your mentee's journey.

- Allows you to hold the mirror without projection and supports mapping without control.

- Builds the inner maturity needed to meet mentees where they are, not where you think they *should* be.

Final Thought

Being a holistic mentor is not about having all the answers. It's about having the inner spaciousness to hold for yourself and others. Mirror and Map is more than a tool—it's a way of being and living that transforms how you guide others by guiding yourself.

References:

Argyris, Chris. "Teaching Smart People How to Learn." *Harvard Business Review* 69, no. 3 (May–June 1991): 99–109.

Kristen Dombrowski, PCC, CPCC, is deeply committed to living and leading on purpose with intention. As a mother, entrepreneur, and unwavering learner, she has spent much of her life exploring how we grow, connect, and show up—especially when things are messy or uncertain. Whether personal or professional, Kristen strives to bring deep listening, honest reflection, and a sense of groundedness. Her roles continue to teach her how to slow down, stay open, and embrace the process.

With over 25 years of experience in learning and development and a master's degree in organizational psychology, Kristen brings a thoughtful blend of curiosity, empathy, and resilience. Drawn to the inner world of people, she uses the Mirror and Map tool to walk with leaders, teams, and women navigating change to find clarity, alignment, and meaning in work and lives.

Kristen's work as a coach, facilitator, and consultant is grounded in emotional intelligence, mindfulness, and relationship-building—but at its core, it's about being present with people as they discover what matters most to them and how to use that to live a more fulfilled, conscious, balanced life.

Kristen supports:

- Leaders who want to grow from the inside out—building emotional intelligence, deepening self-awareness, and leading with integrity.
- Teams seeking stronger relationships, clearer communication, and a more human-centered culture.
- Women in transition—professionally or personally—who are ready to reclaim their voice, vision, and value.

She is certified in a range of tools, including Hogan, EQ-i, MBTI, SDI, and the Enneagram, and uses them to help uncover strengths, values, and blind spots. But her work always begins with the human being in front of her—not just the role or goal.

For Kristen, growth is an inside-out journey—and no one has to walk it alone.

Connect with Kristen:

Website: https://www.kristendombrowski.com

LinkedIn: https://www.linkedin.com/in/kristen-dombrowski/

Facebook: https://www.facebook.com/leadliveonpurpose/about/

CHAPTER SEVEN

MY AGE AND STAGE ARE MY SUPERPOWER

OVERCOMING IMPOSTER SYNDROME AS A NEXT-GEN MENTOR

Kristin A. Goodrich

One generation shall commend your works to another
and shall declare your mighty acts.

~ Psalm 145:4 (ESV)

Sweaty palms. Knotted stomach. Teary eyes.

Who among us hasn't been crippled by fear? Who hasn't felt the burden of our finger-wagging, sarcastic inner voice yelling, "Faker! Imposter!"

Yet haven't you risen above the challenge?

Taken a test and passed it, whether barely or with flying colors?

Walked to the edge of the high dive, stepped off, and then free-fell to the pool below?

Got hard, unwelcome news for yourself or a loved one, and found yourself standing faithful and true?

Regardless of age or stage, we've faced and met the challenges set before us, kicking our faulty imposter syndrome thinking to the curb. Let us not hoard our hard-won lessons, but let us encourage the next generation to surpass us in virtuous leadership.

MY STORY

"Stop if someone points a gun at you."

Just five days after leaving the classroom, I faced my real-life final exam amidst the thrum of low-flying helicopters, the plumes of white and black smoke, red tracers arcing across the night sky, and the rat-a-tat-tat of live ammunition fire.

Panamanian dictator General Manuel Noriega had recently declared war on the United States, and the U.S. responded by invading Panama.

Marine Warrant Officer Charlie Rowe sat in the front passenger seat of the white U.S. Navy van as I drove, calmly having me do what he so easily could have done himself.

"Don't stop for the red lights."

"Drive slowly up to the roadblock and look for *friend* or *foe*."

My public affairs training was designed to maximize distance between the media and military operations, born from deeply seated distrust during the Vietnam War.

Charlie showed up, sharing with me his graduate-level public affairs expertise learned in Lebanon and Panama. As the technical expert, he helped me navigate the challenge of embedding novice journalists and me into this new jungle combat zone:

- When we drove over the Bridge of the Americas, with snipers hanging from the girders, ferrying journalists eager to get to the street fighting
- When inexperienced camera crews kept getting in the line of fire, hoping for a prize-winning photo
- When the panicked sportswriter from the *New York Post* stood up and began walking down the street in an attempt to get away from the chaos of combat

In the following months, Charlie continued to provide the mentorship I didn't even know I needed or could have. Instead of letting me be crippled by my imposter syndrome, he beckoned me forward and I was able to perform beyond the expectations of my young age and early life stage.

GROWING PAST IMPOSTER SYNDROME TO BECOMING A MENTOR

I'm now a 58-year-old woman with decades of "firsts"—milestones checkered with failures and successes. Make no mistake, the voice of imposter syndrome tried to overshadow confidence and lessons learned during my "laboratory of life" experiences, whispering:

You barely got into the U.S. Naval Academy.

Yet, I graduated with the tenth class of women in May 1989.

You've never had a paycheck in nonprofit work.

Yet, I have decades of experience leading and revitalizing nonprofits, from the local to the international level.

You're too old and irrelevant to offer anything to the next generation.

Yet, the next gen is hungry for mentorship and wants to hear from those who have "been there and done that".

WORK DECISIONS =
TECHNICAL EXPERTISE + THE EMERGING MENTOR

Once we returned to peacetime operations, I published the base news, covered community events, and photographed promotion ceremonies. I immersed myself in the local military faith community, enjoyed eating tropical fruits while lounging in a hammock, and traveled part of the Panama Canal. As a youth group leader, I spent time with high schoolers, not realizing I was becoming a mentor, encouraging the next generation to lead and serve virtuously.

My next wildly different assignment was as a Port Services Officer. I was in charge of the White Beach facility in Okinawa, Japan. Unlike Panama, I had no training for this position. My lack of technical expertise became glaringly apparent the day an amphibious assault ship caused close to half a million dollars of damage to the pier. I would have given my right hand for a mentor to walk alongside me.

Still, I enjoyed experiencing Japanese culture through adult eyes, having spent half my childhood in Tokyo. Little did I know that an unexpected phone call regarding my next assignment would further teach me about mentoring.

Brrrinnggg, brrringg, brrringggg.

Is that the phone ringing at two a.m.?

"Yes?" I groggily answered.

"Ma'am?" asked an annoyed voice.

Not bothered by the fact that she called from an opposite time zone, the officer told me I was assigned to a highly sought-after job in the Naval Academy's admissions office. My job was to master the labyrinthine application process, which I found so challenging.

I supported applicants from nine northeastern states and used my technical expertise to improve the application process for U.S. citizens living abroad. Daily, I spoke with students, parents, administrators, and my region's Blue and Gold Officers (BGOs). I used this opportunity to hone my superpower skills, becoming the mentor I always needed.

SCHOOL DECISIONS =
YOUNG ADULT LIFE – THE MISSING MENTOR

As a high school senior, my imposter syndrome narrative began when I was accepted to the Naval Academy on Memorial Day weekend. I believed—wrongly—I was the last candidate accepted and must have been the least qualified person among 1,350 incoming freshmen.

Part of the application process involved working with a BGO, who is trained by the Naval Academy to inform students about the complicated application process, which can be confusing. The BGO's job was to conduct my interview, speak with school administrators, and coordinate with a coach to evaluate my physical fitness. But he didn't mentor me.

As I arrived on the hallowed school grounds, I continued to hope no one would ever guess I barely got into the academy. Decades later, my Navy classmate, Rita, told the story of how over 30 women were added to our class around the same Memorial Day weekend, to boost the acceptance rate from 100 women to ten percent of the incoming class. News of this truth at long last silenced my faulty imposter narrative.

Throughout those four years of trials and achievements, I longed for an older Christian military woman to serve as my mentor. I treasured the friendships I made with my fellow Academy midshipmen, but I longed for a mentor to challenge, encourage, and guide me.

VOLUNTEERISM DECISIONS =
SKILLS DEVELOPMENT + THE NEW MENTOR

After leaving the Navy, I volunteered as a BGO, conducting hundreds of candidate interviews. Frustrated by the inability of the next generation to carry on a conversation, I found myself wanting to offer suggestions and corrections during BGO interviews. However, I couldn't do so and maintain my integrity. I resigned and voluntarily began to craft a basic interview skills rubric to address word density and verbal punctuation.

I also volunteered within my faith community since spiritual formation was foundational for me. Before long, I moved from attending Bible studies to teaching, then to training the facilitators. I created interactive workshops and loved speaking to groups. Simultaneously, military life introduced me to women who mentored me, enabling me to round out another superpower skill set.

"How?" you ask?

Laurine: You challenged me to face thorny relational patterns, then together we walked through difficult forgiveness and reconciliation journeys.

Laurine saw through my large-and-in-charge adult persona to the little girl with underdeveloped emotional intelligence, needful of therapy and painfully hard work exploring my dysfunctional family system. We've twice walked through the pain of our friendship's implosion; now, we cherish our third and richest chapter, as Laurine lives with stage IV brain cancer.

Brenda: You called out leadership skills in me that fit opportunities at the international level of the PWOC (Protestant Women of the Chapel) *organization.*

Brenda's mentorship began with a wide-ranging conversation on my front porch, followed by her invitation to join the governing body of PWOC International. This invitation allowed me to bring my strategic skills superpower to the team that faced the organization's dismantling. Afterwards, she introduced me to Planting Roots, endorsing me to the leadership team, where I served for eight years as the deputy director.

Amanda and Beth: You accepted the risky yet safe invitation to teach an entire Bible lesson together.

Amanda and Beth locked glances as I passed the sign-up sheet around the Bible study group. Using my mentorship superpower, I drew them into the uncomfortable place of creating an interactive lesson, teaching their peers, and praying aloud. Together, they rose to the occasion, and we still laugh that a snow day forced them to wait an extra week to share what they'd learned.

Today, I have close to 50 years of experience, influenced by mentors, from which to test theories for personal living, examine root causes for my failures and successes, and relax into being the "fearfully and wonderfully made" human I am, as King David described in Psalm 139:14 (ESV).

THE STRATEGY

MISSING:

Mentors

Today's next-gen leaders search for mentors, yet the wait can be years long. Would you consider courageously stepping up as a mentor for a deserving, eager next-gen leader?

Your imposter voice may be whispering doubt and indifference to your soul.

I'm too _____ and too _____ (fill in the blank).

Do you know how badly I've messed up? No way.

Be a mentor? Heck, I need to be mentored!

Mentoring from experience says:

- You've formed good habits that became healthy practices.
- You've faced challenging times and failed.
- You want the next generation to address systemic and complex problems.

Next-gen leaders are interested in enhancing their leadership skills, have questions about guarding their character in turbulent environments, and want to develop technical expertise. Become the mentor you can be, and the one these young leaders need. Difference makers, who are mentors just like you, are grounded in requisite virtues summarized by the Severn Leadership Group's LITER acronym.

Love – Integrity – Truth – Excellence – Relationship

LOVE: YOUR AGE AND STAGE ARE IDEAL

In my 20s, I could have pre-determined I was too young or too inexperienced to mentor others. Had I done so, I would have missed out on making a life-changing difference in the lives of more than one terrified sportswriter from the *New York Post*. As the youth group leader, I cheered at swim meets and ballgames, cried during school musicals, made late-night ice cream runs, and spent hours on the phone listening to teenage drama.

As I prepared to leave Panama, laughter at my farewell party abruptly evaporated when one teen tearfully shared about what I thought was a casual Saturday afternoon phone call. The loving interest she felt from me prompted her to flush a bottle's worth of pills she was just about to swallow.

I was young. I was inexperienced. And I made a difference.

Today, I lovingly give my time and energy to listen to next-gen leaders. I mentor Caroline, a recent graduate of the Naval Academy, among others. For instance, we talk through the challenges of managing relationships with friends and family now scattered across the globe.

"What's the latest with your friend in South Carolina?" I asked her recently.

"Well, she texted a few times, but then things went silent."

"You know she might not have access to her phone while she's working in the secure facility, right?"

"Yes, but the last couple of lines were kinda abrupt."

Gently, I probed the possibilities of what might be going on that day, if Caroline read the text with the worst-case scenario tone of voice, and whether she operated within unstated expectations. I affirmed Caroline's desire to express love to her friend by continuing to reach out every few days.

IMPOSTOR SYNDROME—BETTER YET, SHARE IT

By sharing the ways you've messed up or failed, you diminish the seductive little lies that you are precluded from mentorship. Instead, you're exhibiting integrity when you share transparently about your challenges.

Perhaps you believe searching for an online article detailing "Ten Ways to Deal with a Difficult Boss" replaces the need for virtuous mentors. Unfortunately, the clickbait nature of search engines has no means of discerning the truth of such suggestions, nor any mention of the author's character or behavior in dealing with their difficult boss.

"Brigit, are you focusing on the boss's leadership failures? What if they're differences rather than failures? Is this really your pride talking?

"Where could your emotional response and your rational mind meet? What does wisdom look like here?

"I'm going to poke you: Is this a need or a want?"

Spending years getting to know Brigit, being interested in the details of her situation, and staying at the edge of the dynamic at her work gives me the window into her world—something AI can't match.

"KG, tell me what you notice. I want you to speak the truth in love to me. It's why you're my mentor."

Brigit wants to lead well, and she needs to do so with integrity, and she loves my truthful input.

EXCELLENCE: ANSWER THE HEARTFELT CALL FROM NEXT-GEN LEADERS

If an "A" is perfection, then a "B" is excellence.

Only one perfect person has ever lived, and I'm not Him.

For a long time, I tried to live as close to perfection as possible. Imagine my relief when I discovered the Pareto Principle (above), then personalized my catchphrase of, "80-20 is good enough!"

An 80% is still a "B" and gave me the means to celebrate excellence in the bulk of my work—relationally, professionally, physically, and spiritually. I don't have to be the nearly perfect mentor, nor do I worry about my robustly imperfect life.

As a young leader, I regularly compelled others to work at my hyper-productive output level within volunteer organizations. I demanded near-perfect work from capable leaders with busy lives. As I decreased the pressure, I began to appreciate and even celebrate the team's quality achievements.

A recent concussion, made worse by previous brain injuries, allowed me to personally practice the Pareto Principle as I now have a new, likely permanent, output model nowhere close to perfection.

Remember: Next-gen leaders seek excellent mentors rather than near-perfect ones.

RELATIONSHIPS: BE THE DIFFERENCE MAKER YOUR YOUNGER SELF LONGED TO HAVE

Charlie. Laurine. Brenda. Or Nobody.

What if Charlie didn't teach me to maneuver through the Panamanian countryside? How would I have captioned photos of "prisoners-of-war" or "detainees," describing armed Panamanians who surrendered? Would I have supervised the taking of forensic photos of the Marine who died in combat after a bullet pierced his throat?

What if Laurine didn't share, "Kristin, I think you need to see a counselor. What you're describing about your mother is abuse." I might have continued my destructive relational behaviors. Instead, I learned to label emotions, confess my wrong choices, and apologize. Surprisingly, I have used that growth to reconcile with Laurine. Twice.

What if Brenda didn't spend a Kansas afternoon discussing the meaning of a "sea change," thousands of miles from Navy ships and an ocean? I would have missed multiple professional opportunities with female Christian military leaders. Working so close together, we often burst out laughing with one-line insider comments we instantly understood.

Amanda and Beth epitomize the relationships built when we invite a less experienced, uncertain potential leader into the mentoring space. Amanda prayed aloud and learned about love languages, even as she squirmed when words of affirmation were spoken over her. Beth was moved by the endorsement Laurine and I gave as a reference in her next-step leadership opportunity. I taught Amanda's son to prepare content in bullet form, improve his content through word density, and end his sentences with confidence during college interviews.

Emotionally healthy, problem-solving, virtuous leaders who live within the LITER model are exactly the mentors from whom the next generation longs to hear.

Remember your superpowers:

- Your age and stage are ideal.
- Set aside your "imposter syndrome." Better yet, share about it.

- Answer the heartfelt call from next-gen leaders.
- Be the difference maker your younger self longed to have.

You, too, can take that first, small step and become a next-gen mentor.

Kristin Goodrich is a 1989 graduate of the U.S. Naval Academy and likely the first of her class to serve in combat. As an Air Force wife and mom, she homeschooled her three children in Georgia, Maryland, Germany, Alabama, Texas, and Kansas. Kristin has served at the executive level and on several boards of directors for Christian military ministries.

Known as "KG," her favorite moments include "aha" realizations when someone younger "gets" and accepts a new thought, application, or challenge as a result of a mentoring relationship. Her ability to provide personalized feedback has helped dozens of students succeed in their applications to service academies and ROTC programs.

Born in Brazil and raised in Japan, Colombia, Sweden, and New Jersey, Kristin loves languages, reading fiction, studying history, and strategic thinking. Despite a large and inflexible body, KG started taking classical ballet classes at age 50. She has been married for over 30 years, loves watching her adult children thrive, and delights in the role of grandmother.

KG has been blessed through the mentoring journey and longs for more mentors to encourage our dynamic and accomplished next-gen leaders.

Connect with KG:

LinkedIn: https://www.linkedin.com/in/kristin-goodrich-1950449/

CHAPTER EIGHT

FROM LEADER TO MENTOR

GIVE BACK AND CHANGE LIVES

Donald W. Vinci

I want to give back—maybe do some mentoring. But what does it take to be a mentor? I've never really had one. Sure, I'm a pretty good leader; I've given advice and gotten some too. But that's not really the same, is it?

Sound familiar? You're not alone; it's how I felt when I first thought about mentoring.

MY STORY

Late in my career, a series of emotional and profound events occurred in a few short months that *changed me*, and in time, inspired me to give back through mentorship.

For much of my life, I had no formal mentors and did little mentoring. I did, however, develop leadership skills through experience, readings, and formal training. Of course, other leaders also provided sound advice and support. Little did I realize that so many leadership lessons would one day apply to mentorship.

Later, when my career was at a crossroads, a mentor played a critical role. It wasn't a formal mentorship program, but rather a professional relationship, developed over time, with a senior-level company adviser.

I wasn't selected for a job I really wanted—a senior level position with a big title.

Why? My boss and other senior leaders told me I was one of the best candidates. The person picked was good but had much less leadership experience. Was I misled? Where do I go now? Should I start looking outside?

My mentor talked me through the disappointment of being passed over by asking simple questions. Showing care and compassion, she helped me realize the job wasn't right for me. It was a big, public-facing political role that really didn't fit my personality. I would have been miserable. *She's so right; be patient and keep doing your job. Good things will come.*

Just a couple of months later, I was asked to lead a company-wide cost-cutting initiative. I didn't want the job; it would result in layoffs, turmoil, and take an emotional toll on me and people throughout the company. After several discussions with our CEO, I reluctantly agreed to take it.

In the next month, I recruited two mid-level managers to help lead this critical initiative. They were young and motivated, with incredible potential. I was impressed with them. We spent December planning kickoff meetings for the full team just after the new year.

Over the holidays, I went to the doctor. An ulcer developed on my tongue after a broken tooth, but it never healed.

When the ENT doc looked at my tongue, he said, "That looks very angry. We need to do a biopsy right now." I sat in the chair, mouth open, and couldn't say anything. *That doesn't sound good,* I thought; nodded my head, and just grunted, "Uh-huh."

A couple of days later, I got the call from the doctor. He was direct and to the point. "It's not good news. It's cancer." My head dropped into my hands. I know he said a lot more, but honestly, I don't remember. All I could think was, *What happens now? How do I break this to my wife? My kids?*

Within days, I was diagnosed with stage four squamous cell carcinoma. Scans showed the tumor on my tongue was large, and cancer had spread to my lymph nodes.

Two weeks later, surgeons cut out the cancerous tumor, rebuilt my tongue, and removed lymph nodes from my neck. The next day, I was immobile in the hospital bed, feeding tube in my nose and breathing through a trach tube. The doctor arrived smiling and shared the news we prayed for: "Pathology results are back, and your lymph nodes are clean. The cancer has not metastasized!"

My eyes welled up, and my wife squeezed my hand. That meant no radiation, no chemo, and, by the grace of God, full recovery! I was back to work six weeks later.

In the meantime, my team moved forward to launch that cost-cutting initiative. Those two young mid-level managers laid the groundwork, and together we successfully led its implementation. In just a few months, that success changed the trajectory of their careers and helped me land in the C-suite as head of human resources. I was so grateful for their commitment and support, personally and professionally. In fact, through this entire period, the well wishes and help I received from all quarters of my work family were overwhelming.

After years of reflection, I know this series of events—from the mentor who guided me after deep disappointment to the incredible people who supported and helped me through my cancer diagnosis—*changed me.* When I was most vulnerable, others held me up. I had to find a way to give back and do the same. Mentoring was one of those ways.

THE STRATEGY

In my experience, three principles best describe a mentor's role, mindset, and behaviors. Their attributes are based on leadership lessons I apply directly to my role as a mentor. Practicing these principles results in a healthy mentor-mentee relationship and effective mentee development.

Principle One: Show up with the right mindset; it starts with them and is all about them.

It's critical to be authentic and develop trust quickly. You want the relationship to become that of a peer or colleague. As we say at the Severn Leadership Group (SLG), "Walk beside your mentee."

Nothing builds trust more quickly and effectively than demonstrating you care. I'm sure you've experienced this.

When I was a young junior officer on a nuclear submarine, my commanding officer, Captain More, did something that both surprised me and immediately established a high level of trust and commitment to him as a leader. It was the height of the Cold War, and while headed out to sea, we got word that my grandmother had died. I remember feeling sad but resigned to reality: *I'm a submariner and submariners don't get humevac'ed* (the Navy term for evacuating personnel for humanitarian reasons).

Captain More, on the other hand, did just that. He requested and received permission to delay our arrival to the assigned patrol area, surface the ship, and humevac me. He demonstrated he cared—to me and the entire crew. It's a leadership lesson I'll always remember—a lesson in caring that applies directly to mentorship.

How can you show caring and develop trust with a mentee? One simple thing is to connect them to your network.

For example, a mentee who worked in the IT field established a small group of IT professionals to partner with business units at her company. When I offered to connect her to a former colleague and senior IT leader for advice, she looked up and opened her mouth. I could hear her inhale. "That would be great!" She was so appreciative and received great advice from an industry expert. And, importantly, that simple act of caring quickly established trust between us.

In another instance, I mentored a college student who struggled to discover herself and the direction to start her career. She didn't know what she wanted. I put her in touch with folks at my company who hire intern engineers for summer work. She applied and was accepted.

A couple of years later, we caught up over lunch. She was in a great mood, and as we talked, I thought, *She's really matured.* Reminiscing about the last few years, her voice pitch went up a couple of notes. Chuckling, she said, "When we first met, I was so scattered—I didn't know what I wanted to do! Now, I feel so different. That time as an intern made all the difference."

A small act of caring on my part built significant trust with someone I stay in touch with to this day.

Of course, there are many other ways to show up for them, but the key is to maintain the right mindset. Regardless of how your discussions go, what tangents they may take, or even how frustrated you sometimes feel, remind yourself they're on a developmental journey. Meet them where they are—it's all about them.

Principle Two: Let them grow; empower mentees to invest in the process and self-learn.

Good leaders help their people grow and can empower them through effective engagement. Listen carefully and ask probing questions to seek understanding and reveal gaps in their thought processes or plans. Use this leadership lesson to put the second principle into practice.

Late in my career, our company's chief information officer reported directly to me but supported and worked for the entire executive team. He made many presentations to the group.

A few months into my tenure, he said to me, "Don, thank you for being so interested in what we're doing in IT. When I present at executive team meetings, some of the others are distracted or silent. You always listen, ask questions, and make me think. When we meet one-on-one to discuss an issue or initiative, I have to be ready because you're going to ask good questions."

I thought, *Oh no, I hope he doesn't think I don't trust him or that I'm trying to micromanage.* I thanked him for the feedback and said, "I'm asking all those questions because I'm trying to learn the IT world, something I don't have much experience with." He said, "Yes, and it's so helpful! You help me see things I didn't consider. I learn from that."

In my experience, listening intently and asking good questions are critical skills to help lead your mentee on a path of self-learning and growth.

For example, if your mentee doesn't know what areas to work on or struggles to articulate developmental needs, ask probing, open-ended questions to help them think it through. Start with "what" questions:

"What's your biggest challenge? What are you most worried about? What feedback have you gotten from your boss, colleagues, or subordinates?"

Then follow up with "why" questions:

"Why is that? Why do you think they said or did that? Why is that important?"

In the end, they will more clearly identify how to benefit from mentorship; perhaps specify two or three goals. Or something less concrete—maybe they just need a sounding board to help work through professional or personal challenges.

Now, unfortunately, a good mentor can easily undermine this second principle by being too quick to provide advice. It's something I struggle with to this day.

Most mentees enter a mentoring relationship seeking advice—and yes, you will likely provide that along the way. However, your approach will be much more effective if it helps a mentee self-learn by requiring them to invest in the process, grapple through their thoughts, and identify next steps—not hand them an answer in the form of advice.

Here's one of the best techniques I've found to resist jumping to advice. When your mentee describes a struggle or challenge, and you start thinking, *Oh, I've been there myself. I know what she should do next:* stop! Instead, think, *What questions should I ask?*

I once had a mentee say, "Don, can I get your advice on something? My team and I are falling short of revenue targets. We rely on the sales team to bring in business. So, I had a meeting with one of the sales reps to understand what support they needed and how I might help. His boss also participated in the meeting. After asking a few questions, the sales rep cut me off. 'I'm sorry, I just don't have the bandwidth to help you.' I was stunned. Even worse, his boss didn't say anything! I didn't know what to do with this."

As he talked, my mind started formulating the advice he sought: *You've got to follow up with this guy and set up a meeting with his boss.* But then, I stopped myself. *Wait, what questions should I ask? What will help him think through the next steps?* So, we went back and forth.

"Well, that's a pretty bad situation. What have you thought about doing?"

"I don't know. After a couple days stewing over it, I kinda just decided to let it drop, but it's just not right." He threw up his hands, sighed, and dropped his shoulders.

"So, maybe you shouldn't let it drop?"

He shook his head, "Yeah, you're right. I need to follow up with that sales rep."

"Before you do that, do you have any idea why he might have responded that way?"

"I don't know, but he didn't seem to have a problem saying it in front of his boss."

"Have you thought about talking with his boss?"

His body language changed. He sat up straight and looked right at me. "No, I hadn't thought about that. That's a good idea. I don't know what his boss expects from him."

"Do you know if this sales rep has had performance issues in the past?"

"I do think there have been issues in the past. I can ask his boss about that, too." He was taking notes.

He left our discussion with a much clearer path forward and confident that it was the right approach. It was *his* plan.

Ask good questions and resist just giving advice. Empower your mentee to grow through self-discovery and learning.

Principle Three: Be engaged; actively support them throughout the journey.

Leaders support their people in many ways. I've mentioned several: demonstrate you care, connect them to your network, show interest, ask good questions.

Another way is by holding others accountable. To be effective, expectations must be set and agreed upon upfront, followed by regular check-ins with honest, early discussions if things go off track. I've found *The Oz Principle* by Craig Hickman and Roger Connors an invaluable resource for implementing a healthy, supportive culture of accountability.

Apply leadership lessons in accountability to mentorship. If your mentee identifies developmental goals and/or specific actions, offer to be an accountability partner. It will help them prioritize their time and invest in the process.

Most importantly, leaders support their people by providing honest and effective feedback—constructive feedback when needed, and sincere positive reinforcement at every opportunity.

There are several feedback models out there, and leaders and mentors should become skilled at providing feedback. I won't detail them here, but I highly recommend two. The Center for Creative Leadership teaches the SBII model, where the person giving feedback describes the situation and behaviors observed and then questions or discusses the intent versus the impact of those behaviors. Similarly, the Severn Leadership Group teaches the CCI model (Context, Conduct, Intent) as described in Sig Berg's book *The Virtue Proposition: Five Virtues That Will Transform Leadership, Team Performance, and You.* You can find it in the resources section below.

Mentees need feedback; it's the lifeblood of a mentoring relationship. As a mentor, you may be their only source of honest feedback. They frequently struggle, are hard on themselves, and get frustrated. Sometimes, they need to vent; let them. It may not be the time for feedback. Other times, they need feedback in the form of perspective.

Once, I was down, disappointed in myself, and struggling, thinking, *I don't understand what I did wrong. What did I say or do that caused that kind of reaction? I've tried to fix it, but nothing is working.* I stewed on it for days, losing sleep at night. When I talked it through with my mentor, she said, "Don, it's a great big life." She said a lot more, but that phrase stuck and helped me move past it.

Don't miss an opportunity to provide positive feedback; it motivates, energizes, and gives a mentee confidence. I started mentoring a mid-level manager as part of the SLG Fellows leadership development program. During one of our first meetings, we briefly discussed the importance of self-awareness and blind spots. I told him, "You'll learn more about this in one of the program's future sessions."

At our very next meeting, he told me, "Don, I thought a lot about our last discussion, so I put together a little survey and sent it to my team. I asked them to tell me what I was doing well and what I should work on. I've already gotten a few responses."

I kinda got chills. *Are you kidding me? The first time we discuss something meaty, and you do all that! It's not a homework assignment for the SLG program, but maybe it should be.*

I said to him, "Michael, that just blows me away. You took something we discussed briefly to heart and turned it into action. I can't tell you how impressed I am. Not only are you getting great feedback to help with your development, but think about the message it sends to your team. They know you're committed to improving and want their help." As I talked, his smile got bigger and bigger; he beamed.

There you have it. Three mentor principles based on leadership lessons:

1. Show up with the right mindset; it starts with them and is all about them.

   • Be authentic

   • Demonstrate you care

   • Build trust

2. Let them grow; empower mentees to invest in the process and self-learn.

   • Help them define what they want out of the relationship

   • Actively listen and ask good questions

   • Resist the urge to offer advice too quickly

3. Be engaged; actively support them throughout the journey.

   • Be their accountability partner

   • Provide honest and effective feedback

   • Utilize the power of positive reinforcement

Events in my life changed and inspired me to give back by mentoring others. Apply these three principles and become a great mentor – you will change lives.

Resources

Berg, Sig. *The Virtue Proposition*. Amplify Publishing, 2024.

Donald W. Vinci is an accomplished C-suite executive who retired from Entergy Corporation (a Fortune 300 company) after a successful career leading both operational and corporate functions. He served for more than five years on the executive leadership team, first as Chief Human Resources Officer and then as Executive Vice President and Chief Administrative Officer. He served on active duty as a submarine officer for more than six years and in the Navy Reserves for 17 years, retiring as a captain in 2003.

A strategic thinker and lifelong learner who thrived in difficult and challenging situations, Don served in diverse and varied leadership positions—from demanding and unforgiving environments as a nuclear submarine officer and later as plant manager in the commercial nuclear industry, to broad business roles where he led Entergy's risk management services and gas distribution business.

Don enjoys traveling to visit grandkids, playing music, golf, and has become an avid sailor. He's also giving back as a board member, mentor, and facilitator for the Severn Leadership Group (SLG). He serves on advisory boards for Tulane University's School of Science and Engineering and the NROTC Alumni Association.

Don is married to his high school sweetheart and is a proud father of two accomplished daughters. He's a New Orleans native and received a bachelor's degree in chemical engineering and a master's degree in business administration, both from Tulane University. He was a licensed professional engineer in Louisiana and a licensed senior reactor operator at the Waterford 3 nuclear station.

Connect with Don:
LinkedIn: https://www.linkedin.com/in/don-vinci-b08411
Email: don.vinci@severnleadership.org

PART: 3

CREATING SPACE FOR GROWTH

CHAPTER NINE

BUILDING BRIDGES

THE ART OF AUTHENTIC CONNECTION

Kristen Whitley, Certified Coach and Mentor

When we are seen, we are healed.
When we are heard, we are empowered.
When we are connected, we are unstoppable.

~ Unknown

MY STORY

This woman is a warrior with combat experience. How much value can I bring to her?

In preparation for a new session of the SLG Fellows Program, I met for the first time with my assigned fellow: an accomplished navy officer preparing for her first department head tour. I read her biography and LinkedIn profile and was honestly a bit intimidated. Although I'm also a former navy officer and attended the same college she did, we had vastly different careers.

My jobs in the Navy were largely administrative. Positions like hers weren't even available to women when I served.

But as I opened our first Zoom call, I immediately noticed Morgan had great difficulty making eye contact.

Something's off.

She seemed to be staring down and to the left as we greeted each other. I had to turn up the volume on my computer speaker to hear her clearly as she told me about her family, current job situation, and goals for her time in the fellowship cohort. Her voice and body language in no way matched her accomplishments. Rather than being intimidated, I was puzzled. Something was clearly off.

Morgan needed someone in her life who could help her recognize her strengths and embody her abilities. *Could I be that person?*

With a holistic approach to mentorship, the SLG Fellows Program had the potential to be exactly what Morgan needed. Although she previously worked with other mentors in the Navy, those individuals were primarily focused on helping her develop her career by selecting key assignments and navigating leadership challenges in her jobs.

Morgan doesn't really need a coach with extensive technical expertise in her field; she needs a mentor and a program that can help her become a better version of herself and develop a greater sense of her own well-being.

The SLG Fellows Program offered everything she needed; my challenge as her mentor was to connect with her deeply enough to help her apply the material and discussions, and then develop a plan to increase her overall life satisfaction and confidence in living a life of purpose and meaning.

The first step was to help Morgan feel safe enough to share her whole story: not just the information she would include in a professional biography, but the deeper, more weighty story of her life experiences and current concerns. As I gave Morgan an overview of the contents of the SLG program, I emphasized that anything discussed during our mentor sessions and in the larger cohort sessions was confidential.

"Morgan, I want to assure you that anything you share with me will never be repeated to anyone else. To get the most out of your mentorship, it is important that you feel comfortable discussing everything that may impact your overall well-being. Likewise, in our large group sessions, the other mentees and mentors will be discussing their own challenges and real-world problems, so we ask that you keep those confidences as well. The SLG Program is a safe space for all."

To illustrate this point, I told Morgan my own story. I made sure to emphasize some of the most difficult times I faced as a woman in the military, a partner in a troubled first marriage that ultimately ended in divorce, and later as a professional working wife and mother struggling to balance career, marriage, and children. As I finished telling my story, I noticed Morgan was now completely engaged; she looked directly into my eyes and even smiled. Her whole countenance was different.

"Kristen, thank you so much. I didn't know what to expect out of this program, but I am so glad you are my mentor. I feel really comfortable talking to you, and I think this is really going to help me. I love that we share some similar experiences, and I am really excited to meet the other members of our group."

As Morgan and I walked together through her SLG Fellowship, she faced some huge personal challenges. She struggled in her marriage and dealt with some significant health issues that could result in her separation from the Navy. Morgan planned to make the military her career, and now her future was in the hands of a medical review board that could end that career—or perhaps allow her to stay in, but on a restricted status, making her ineligible for command at sea. She didn't know if she was going to her next assignment on a new ship or if she would be looking for a new job as a civilian. She also didn't know if her husband would join her or if she would face her future alone. As her mentor, I provided a safe place for her to discuss these issues and explore possibilities.

As we worked through the material in the SLG program, I made notes of Morgan's unique gifts and aptitudes and helped her recognize her strengths. As she shared some of her concerns about her marriage, I suggested she and her husband could benefit from meeting with a marriage counselor, and Morgan could benefit from some counseling to navigate the uncertainty of her future. As someone who also transitioned from the Navy to a civilian career and endured the pain of marital problems, I knew it was critically important for Morgan to identify who she truly was at her core. She was more than just a military officer and wife to her husband; she was a talented, virtuous woman with values, gifts, and leadership abilities that would serve her well no matter what the future held.

> "Kristen, I think the hardest part of this time in my life is the uncertainty. In two months, I could be moving to report to a new job on a brand new ship, I could be transitioning to a completely different job in the Navy where I can't go to sea, or I could be out of the service entirely and looking for a civilian job. I don't even know if I will still be married."

> "I completely understand. You have been in the Navy since you were 18 years old. It is so easy to define ourselves in terms of our roles: 'I am a Navy officer.' 'I am John's wife.' 'I am my parents' daughter.' But you are more than that, Morgan. You are an incredibly intelligent woman with strong leadership skills and a lot of compassion and empathy. You crave challenge and are ambitious, and you want a loving, committed marriage with the ability to have children one day. You can have all of those things, no matter what job or relationship you have. Together, we have drilled down and defined who you are underneath all those roles."

Over the next few months, I introduced Morgan to people in my own network who could speak to her about opportunities in the Navy for individuals with medical restrictions and to colleagues who transitioned from the Navy into successful civilian careers. I encouraged Morgan to reach out to members of her cohort who were currently working in roles that interested her, and to attend job fairs and conferences for military officers transitioning to civilian life. I also provided her with a contact who could help her access disability services through the Veterans' Administration in case she had to leave the service. Together, we operated from the perspective that gathering information and utilizing all resources would empower her during a time when so much seemed out of her control.

Morgan expressed surprise when most of her initial inquiry calls resulted in immediate interviews and job offers. Instead of feeling powerless, she began to feel confident in her ability to successfully face whatever decision the medical board presented. A few months after Morgan's SLG Fellowship Program ended, she texted me to schedule another Zoom call. As I opened the call, a smiling, confident woman greeted me, looking directly into her camera and speaking with authority.

> "Hey Kristen, thanks so much for scheduling this time. I know the fellowship is over, but you said that you were always available for check-ins. I have a tough decision to make, and I just want to talk through it with you."
>
> "Of course, Morgan. It's great to see you. What's going on?"
>
> "Well, the medical board came back and gave me a separation date of November 30th, so it looks like I'll be leaving the Navy."
>
> "How are you feeling about that?"
>
> "Okay. You know, it's been a long time coming, and there's been a lot of uncertainty. I have a great therapist who has really helped me put this in perspective, and mostly I'm just relieved to have this resolved."
>
> "That's great, Morgan. I'm so proud of you."
>
> "Yeah, me too. I'm really at peace with this. My problem is, I have two really great job offers and I'm not sure which one to take."

"Morgan, congratulations! I'm not surprised. I told you you'd have more choices than you knew what to do with! Now, tell me about these opportunities."

Serving as Morgan's mentor was a true privilege and clarified the power of authentic connection. The mentor relationship, built on trust, mutual respect, and intentionality, can empower leaders to become the best possible versions of themselves.

THE STRATEGY

A great mentor is more than just experienced; they're present, invested, and equipped with the skills to support someone else's growth. By applying the following foundational strategies and guiding principles, mentors can make meaningful and lasting connections to impact others' lives.

SERVING AS A MENTOR IS A PRIVILEGE AND MUST BE A PRIORITY

Mentorship is a gift—to both the mentee and the mentor. When someone looks to you for guidance, support, and inspiration, it's a powerful vote of confidence in your character and leadership. Treating the role as a privilege reminds you to show up with purpose and commitment. This means carving out time, following through on promises, and genuinely caring about your mentee's development. Good mentors don't treat these interactions as optional or secondary to "more important" work. They understand that connecting and investing in others is one of the most important contributions they can make.

ESTABLISH PSYCHOLOGICAL SAFETY

Before connection can happen, you must build trust. A mentee must feel safe sharing their goals, fears, and uncertainties. Creating psychological safety involves being nonjudgmental, empathetic, and receptive. It requires you to be intentional about your tone, responses, and openness.

Be mindful of your facial expressions and body language to ensure they convey open, relaxed, attentive listening. Keep responses thoughtful and supportive rather than critical or trite. Aim to cultivate an environment where your mentee knows their thoughts are valued, and their vulnerabilities won't be used against them.

ENSURE CONFIDENTIALITY AND BE WILLING TO BE VULNERABLE YOURSELF

Confidentiality is the backbone of a successful mentoring relationship. When a mentee shares personal information, professional frustrations, or career aspirations, they are trusting you with sensitive material. Guard this trust fiercely. Be clear at the outset that what is shared stays between you. Also, don't shy away from being vulnerable yourself. Sharing your own challenges, insecurities, and lessons learned not only humanizes you but also encourages the mentee to be open as well. Vulnerability invites vulnerability—and it's in this shared space that real connection and growth happen.

PREPARE FOR EVERY CALL OR MEETING

Preparation signals respect. Before every session, review notes from previous meetings, reflect on what you discussed, and consider how you can best support your mentee's current needs. This may involve doing research, identifying resources, or simply preparing thoughtful questions. Your preparedness helps maintain focus and demonstrates you're not just showing up—you're showing up for them.

PAY ATTENTION. NO DISTRACTIONS. PRACTICE ACTIVE LISTENING WITHOUT INTERRUPTING

Being fully present is perhaps the most underrated mentoring skill. In today's world, where multitasking is the norm, giving someone your undivided attention is a powerful act of respect. If you're meeting in person, put away phones, close your laptop, and eliminate distractions. For online meetings, ensure that the only screen and window you are using is the one on the call. Practice active listening: make eye contact, nod in acknowledgment, paraphrase what you hear, and refrain from formulating your response while the mentee is still speaking. When you listen without interrupting, you invite deeper, more thoughtful conversation and give your mentee space to explore their ideas out loud.

TAKE NOTES

Taking notes during or after a session shows that you value what your mentee says and are invested in tracking their progress. It also helps you remember key points, identify patterns over time, and provide more targeted guidance. Let your mentee know you're doing this—not because you're "keeping tabs," but because they matter to you. Simple things like remembering spouses' and children's names convey that you care about their lives and overall well-being.

ASK QUESTIONS

The best mentors don't offer answers—they ask great questions. Good questions help mentees think more deeply, challenge assumptions, and explore new possibilities. Open-ended questions such as "What do you think success looks like here?" or "What are you afraid might happen?" invite introspection and build self-awareness. Resist the urge to problem-solve immediately. Instead, be curious. Ask follow-ups. Your goal is to help your mentee arrive at their own insights, not to impose your own solutions.

SHARE STORIES AS APPROPRIATE, INCLUDING YOUR OWN FAILURES, SETBACKS, AND PERSONAL CHALLENGES

One of the most powerful things you can offer as a mentor is your story—especially the messy parts. Sharing failures, detours, and personal hardships creates connection and credibility. It reminds your mentee that growth is never linear and success is often born out of struggle. Your vulnerability will make it easier for them to process their own setbacks and stay motivated. Just ensure your storytelling is relevant and not dominating the conversation. Stories should support, not eclipse, the mentee's journey.

REFRAIN FROM PROVIDING ADVICE. WE ARE NOT COUNSELORS

While it can be tempting to jump in with advice, especially when you see a clear solution, it's important to remember that mentoring is not counseling. Your job is not to direct someone's life, but to guide them in exploring their options. Advice can be limiting if it's perceived as the "right" answer. Instead, help them clarify their thinking and empower them to make informed decisions. Trust that they're capable of finding their way with the right support.

ENCOURAGE

Everyone benefits from encouragement—especially those at turning points in their careers or facing challenges. A mentor's belief in a mentee can be a powerful catalyst. A kind word, recognition of effort, or even a simple, "I believe in you," can go a long way. Encourage them not only in their successes but also in their resilience, their ability to learn, and their growth over time. Celebrate the process, not just the outcomes.

CHALLENGE

A great mentor doesn't just affirm—they challenge. Encourage your mentee to stretch beyond their comfort zone, question their assumptions, and take healthy risks. Challenging doesn't mean being harsh or critical; it means holding up a mirror and helping them see where they're playing it safe or not living up to their potential. Ask them to set goals, be accountable, and pursue excellence. Growth doesn't happen in complacency.

HELP THEM IDENTIFY THEIR STRENGTHS AND SKILLS

Sometimes people can't see their own strengths until someone points them out. Help your mentee identify and articulate what they do well. Pay attention to recurring themes in your conversations and reflect those back to them. "You're really good at building consensus," or "I've noticed you ask insightful questions" are examples of simple observations that can build confidence and provide direction. As mentees develop a clearer sense of their abilities, they'll be better positioned to apply them purposefully.

PROVIDE ACCESS TO YOUR PROFESSIONAL NETWORK

One of the most valuable gifts a mentor can offer is access. Introduce your mentee to people in your network who can support their goals, offer expertise, or simply expand their worldview. These introductions don't need to lead to immediate opportunities. Even a short conversation with a new contact can be incredibly eye-opening. Help your mentee learn how to network effectively, and model generosity in how you connect others.

In conclusion, mentoring is both a responsibility and a profound opportunity to impact someone's personal and professional journey. By creating a safe and supportive space, listening deeply, asking powerful questions, and offering both challenge and encouragement, mentors can build bridges to connect deeply with others regardless of age, job title, or career field. It requires effort, humility, and consistency—but the rewards, for both the mentee and the mentor, are extraordinary.

Kristen Whitley is a self-employed coach, speaker, and trainer focused on helping individuals and groups achieve greater productivity, interpersonal health, and overall life satisfaction. With a diverse background in leadership roles spanning the military, sales organizations, and education, Kristen offers unique insights into common organizational and personal challenges, leveraging her experiences to provide others with the knowledge, tools, and resources to optimize their performance.

Prior to founding her own business, Kristen most recently served as the Director of Student Services for Foundation Christian Academy in Valrico, Florida. With a vision of helping the school offer private education services to students with learning and developmental disabilities, Kristen established the Special Education program, trained and mentored classroom teachers, and worked with students and parents to develop individualized learning plans.

Before her time in education, Kristen served as the Director of Sales Team Training for a private IT consulting firm, where she was recognized as a top sales producer in business services.

A graduate of the U.S. Naval Academy, Kristen's earliest leadership roles included serving as the Legal Officer for a Navy Fighter Squadron and as the Protocol Officer for the Admiral commanding the U.S. Navy and Marine Corps bases in the San Diego region.

Kristen received a Bachelor of Science degree from the U.S. Naval Academy and a Master's of Education Degree in Teaching and Learning from Liberty University. She is a certified Speaker, Trainer, and Coach with the John Maxwell Leadership Team, and a certified Yoga and Mindfulness Instructor and Continuing Education Provider with Yoga Alliance.

Connect with Kristen:

LinkedIn: https://www.linkedin.com/in/kristen-colbert-whitley/

Email: https://kristencwhitley@gmail.com

CHAPTER TEN

CONNECTING TO YOUR MENTEE

DEEPENING RELATIONSHIPS
BY BECOMING VULNERABLE

Jerome Zazzera, MPT, Mentor, C.S. Lewis Institute

Nothing in all creation is hidden from God's sight.
Everything is uncovered and laid bare before the eyes of him
to whom we must give account.

~ Hebrews 4:13 (ESV)

MY STORY

Oh God, I'm afraid. How much do I share about my sinful past?

Ten minutes until we convene. It's early September, and a new men's cohort is forming for the C.S. Lewis Institute's Discipleship program for fellows. Twelve men gather in a circle under a large oak tree overlooking the scenic cove. Each man settles into his Adirondack chair and tries to settle his nerves.

Each mentee has been aware of this moment for months. As a mentee several years ago, I've been in their shoes and am now recalling my apprehension of sitting in this circle, waiting to give my testimony. The tension is almost palpable. One by one, every man will share his testimony regarding his life before following Jesus and his life after following Jesus. Later in the weekend, each fellow will be paired with his mentor for his year of study.

I can hear the stressful thoughts of each man. How much do I share?

Should I speak in vagueness so I can hide those things about myself I don't want anybody to know about me?

Maybe I can just share half-truths, so I won't be judged.

I feel for these men. I'll ask them to be vulnerable, to take risks in sharing deeply personal things about their behaviors, relationships, and failures. Within me is the great desire for these men to experience tremendous growth in their relationship with Jesus during the year-long fellows program.

My job is to get these men to open up, not only to me but to one another, to feel safe in each other's presence, and to be willing to share the deepest fears and longings in their lives.

How can I facilitate a deep connection among these men? How do I bolster their trust? How can I encourage them to expose their wounds to one another despite any fears they may have about being truly known? In short, how can I create an environment of safety where they'll experience the inner freedom of being vulnerable to one another?

It's time! To begin, I offer the following prayer.

"Come, Holy Spirit. We can do nothing by ourselves. Open the hearts and minds of these men gathered here who desire to grow in their walk with you, Lord Jesus. Help each of us to feel your presence, to trust in your protection, and to be not afraid to share both their successes and failures. Let them know and feel they are safe here in this space. In Jesus' name, amen."

As the facilitator, I offer to give my testimony first. This is the critical first step. If I'm to inspire a culture of sharing deeply those experiences that have caused shame, embarrassment, and failure, I must have the courage to be transparent with these men. In short, I have to become vulnerable to each of these men.

So, I begin. "Hi, I'm Jerry. I grew up in a small town in Carbondale, Pennsylvania. Mom and I had a very close relationship. She was always present to me in my first 17 years of life. Baseball was my passion, and she never missed a game in all those years. She didn't coddle me, and I remember the great life lesson about being honest she taught me at about age eight. We left a store, and I had stolen a box of Junior Mints, which she was unaware of until we got home. Upon seeing the box, she asked me where I got it and how I paid for it. My confession of theft led her to marching me back to the store and apologizing to the store owner. Boy, was I scared!"

"My relationship with my dad was not so good. He wasn't present most of the time. Sadly, he never attended a single one of my ballgames, and no matter what I did in any area of my young life—sports, school, or household chores—it was never good enough."

"High school graduation resulted in my enlistment into the Army and ultimately an appointment to West Point. Through this phase of my life, my relationship with Jesus grew, but I became very arrogant."

Almost without my knowing it, that word, "arrogant," slips out. *My first confession.* I pause and scan the faces for hints of judgment. I can't tell. The Holy Spirit nudges me to continue.

"While I held Jesus as my Lord and Savior, I held myself only slightly below Him. This arrogance led to an ever-increasing sense of pride and superiority over others. My fall from grace was inevitable. My savior complex led me to become involved with a married woman who was in a difficult marriage. She also had three young children."

There, I said it. I confessed my adultery to this new band of brothers. Old emotions of shame, guilt, and embarrassment wash over me. Inside, the war was rekindled. *Don't say too much because they won't respect you. They'll judge you. They'll avoid you.* I feel my body temperature rising, and a cold sweat on my hands.

"Again, because of my pride, I looked at myself as her savior, her rescuer. This adulterous relationship lasted 20 years."

My mind is aghast! *Did I just say 20 years?* At this point, I can feel the old pangs in my heart open the scarred-over wounds anew. I know I must go on, though. There's no stopping this runaway train of letting go and letting the Spirit lead me.

"Many people were speaking truth to me: this relationship was wrong, but I didn't listen. I was so arrogant that I even tried to justify the relationship with scripture. I became King David of the Old Testament, and she was Bathsheba. I falsely reasoned it would work out in the end, as it did for David. It did not. It was a disaster. God finally broke me, and I confessed this grotesque sin, and he restored me."

I conclude my testimony by describing how He restored me and led me to meet my wonderful wife, Angie, with whom I have loved journeying for 19 years.

There it is! My heart lay bare before these diverse men from all ages and backgrounds. I choose to be vulnerable in allowing myself to face my fears of being judged, rejected as a fraud, and a hypocrite. I allow my brokenness and my moral failure to be seen and heard. How will the group respond?

I finish and ask who would like to go next. There's a brief, pregnant silence, and then another man says, "I'll go."

What transpires is an openness to share his failures in life. The next man, and then the next, shares his testimony. These men confess every type of addiction, relationship failure, rebellion against God and others, deception, lying, stealing, coveting, gossip, manipulation, and pride. After these testimonies, there's a lightness in the room. They're no longer bound by the weight of their past sins. Healing has begun. Tense faces and averted eyes are replaced by a softness of expression and eye contact with one another. The foundation has been set for connecting deeply, mentor to mentee.

With vulnerability as the foundation for connecting to a mentee, the next building blocks can be laid. Becoming vulnerable is akin to being a live wire. If not harnessed and shaped with love and compassion, then personal growth may be arrested in the following strategy. Being vulnerable powerfully gets the mentee's attention. Now, the building blocks of active listening, avoiding dictation of what the mentee should do, and refraining from judgment become part of the conversation.

THE STRATEGY

Allow your love and compassion for your mentee to permeate the entire strategy.

VULNERABILITY

What, exactly, is vulnerability? Understanding this concept and allowing oneself to become vulnerable is foundational in cultivating a successful connection to a mentee, upon which a mentor-mentee relationship can flourish throughout the year. This will grow into an abiding friendship based on trust, honesty, and openness. Fundamentally, each of us wants to be known—fully known, as God knows us. At the heart of becoming vulnerable to another is an inner freedom that sheds the pretense of being judged, ridiculed, or afraid. The person can reveal anything about themselves to the other.

ACTIVE LISTENING

The most critical building block is active listening.

1. **Intentional Focus:** Have an intense focus on the mentee whenever they speak. It can be very easy to allow one's mind to drift off onto another topic. If that happens, the mentee will surely notice.

2. **Eye Contact:** Hang on every word spoken by the mentee through consistent eye contact.

Two things often occur at this time. First, an awareness by the mentee begins to form that this person really cares about them. This is not a sterile environment. A friendship is forming that possesses a growing intimacy, but with pristine boundaries. They begin to realize they're sincerely heard. It gives them a correct sense that they're important and their thoughts, opinions, and struggles are important to the mentor. Generally, this leads to more openness and a desire to hear what insights the mentor has to offer regarding the subject you're discussing. Second, an ongoing evaluation and integration of the dialogue happens in real time.

Listening intently provides clues to any underlying problems, priorities, or issues the mentee may have. Organically, through active listening, you ask follow-up questions, giving the mentee pause.

For example, Thomas (not his real name) discusses his struggle with taking the next step in his career, which will require a one-year deployment. When completed, there's a strong possibility he'll be located permanently in one place near his two young daughters, with whom he shares custody with his ex-wife. His problem is that his ex-wife is moving to another state, 1,000 miles away. He has a great relationship with his daughters and is very torn as to what he should do.

Throughout Thomas's sharing, his mentor is demonstrating an intense focus on his every word. He's intent not only on his words, but also on his body language, the anxiety in his eyes, and the sound of significant concern in his voice. Several follow-up questions spawn from his sharing and the active listening.

"How do you feel when the kids aren't present when you get home at night?"

"How invested are you in your current career?"

"Would you consider changing careers if it allowed you more time to share with your children and be an active participant in their development?"

"What other people would be impacted by your decision? Your parents? Your fiancée?"

These are but a few of the questions that developed because the mentor actively listened. Thomas felt listened to, and he realized that each question required careful consideration on his part regarding his priorities going forward. This, then, would ultimately lead to well-thought-out decisions.

NEVER TELL THE MENTEE WHAT TO DO

A critical factor in the above example is that the mentor at no time told the mentee what he should do. I can think of nothing that could hinder the growth of an individual more than using phrases like "You should do this or that."

The mentee's answers to follow-up questions allow them to sift through their thoughts, arriving at decisions resulting from internal analysis. While any decision the mentee makes regarding any topic may be difficult, clarity of thought becomes present. They realize that while any decision may be painful, they know it's the right decision for them in their current circumstance.

All decisions must be the mentee's decisions, not the mentor's. I cannot stress enough how important this self-decision process is to the mentee. They take ownership of their decisions, and it also eliminates any shifting of blame to the mentor.

NO JUDGMENT

Connecting to a mentee can't be achieved if there's a perception by the mentee that they're being judged. Nothing will shut down an open dialogue faster than casting judgment upon a mentee, however slight. Sometimes the mentee is meeting the mentor for the first time, but even when one is known to the other, the mentor must be very careful not to bring their presuppositions, opinions, or beliefs on any subject to the table. To do so sets up barriers to becoming vulnerable, open, and trusting.

For example, suppose the mentee is a leader of a small organization of about 30 people. Through the course of our discussion, it becomes clear that the mentee is a micromanager. He shares with the mentor that several of his employees appear uneasy and unhappy during the organization's day-to-day operations.

If I, as the mentor, go into the conversation with the presupposition that micromanaging is wrong, suppresses creativity, and doesn't allow the employees to use their creative gifts, and I bring my ideas to his attention, then I have, in essence, placed a judgment on how the mentee runs his organization.

My thoughts on how to manage are irrelevant. Perhaps the mentee's particular business requires a certain level of micromanaging, or maybe he feels certain employees are not yet proficient in given areas of the business to allow them more creativity and latitude in their job.

How, then, should a mentor approach such a situation? Maybe the following non-judgmental questions would be helpful. For this example, let us call our mentee George.

"George, tell me about your company. What do you manufacture or what services do you provide?"

This opening question allows the mentee to speak to his passion about his company and his pride in making a laser-designating handgun training device to help gun owners practice their aiming and shooting accuracy without using ammunition. He discusses the cost savings for the buyer and the sense of security it gives buyers to aim and shoot accurately if the need to fire the gun ever arises.

Now, the mentor may have severe reservations about gun ownership and opinions on how guns kill people. If he brings these beliefs up, they'll never get to the reasons behind his employee's uneasiness and unhappiness.

"George, can you describe your manufacturing process?"

Again, I'm getting George to talk about his company's operations.

"It appears the manufacturing process requires a very high level of accuracy. How do you train your employees to meet the high standard of accuracy for your product?"

From here, additional questions about the employee's workstation configuration, quality control procedures, and brainstorming sessions with employees to improve processes can all lead to changes in daily operations that may result in happier employees. At no time is there judgment on his micromanaging or his advocacy for gun ownership despite the mentor's contrary beliefs.

CONCLUSION

Successfully connecting with the mentee can lead to the development of wonderful friendships where two people engage in mutual respect founded on the principles of vulnerability, listening, refraining from dictating what the other should or should not do, and avoiding judgment. Each of these principles works hand in hand with vulnerability as its foundation. Applying these principles leads to increased trust, deeper respect for each other, and the frequent development of enduring friendships.

Jerry Zazzera is a practicing physical therapist in the Baltimore/Annapolis area and a mentor in the C.S. Lewis Institute Fellow's Program at the Annapolis, Maryland chapter. Additionally, both he and his wife, Angie, are active in their church as pre-marital mentors, baptism coordinators, and small group leaders, facilitating people's walk with Jesus. He's stepdad to Jessica and John David, and husband to Angie Jo, a retired nurse who now works in a local barbershop with three other ladies, having great fun cutting men's hair.

Jerry served 11 years in the U.S. Army in various leadership positions in field artillery units, intelligence, special weapons, and new equipment training at the Field Artillery School. This was followed by a 12-year engineering position at Lockheed Corporation, where Jerry worked on various systems for the U.S. Army and NASA. Currently, he's continuing his 28th year of active practice in physical therapy, helping people regain their mobility and return to active lifestyles.

He has a great passion for investing time in one-on-one relationships and helping people discover their particular gifting, and their unique purpose in life.

When he's not engaged in his various mentoring activities or his physical therapy practice, you can find him enjoying hiking, cooking, and traveling with Angie, as well as sharing time with their two granddaughters, Kimberly and Abigail. He loves biking, playing racquetball, and pickleball. He's passionate about studying scripture and leading small group Bible studies with Angie on a variety of topics, with the desire to lead people into deeper relationships with Jesus.

Connect with Jerry:

Email: healingthesacredwound@gmail.com

CHAPTER ELEVEN

MEETING THEM WHERE THEY ARE

HOW TO MAXIMIZE RAPPORT
WITH YOUR MENTEES

James R. McNeal

Leadership is meeting people where they are,
so you can take them where they need to go.

~ Todd Stocker,
Leading from the Gut: 3 Power Principles of Effective Leaders

MY STORY

"I get it now."

"Get what?"

"The Naval Academy's Honor Concept. I finally get it."

Why did it take so long? Adrain was a sophomore, and in addition to a year and a half of living under the Honor Concept at the U.S. Naval Academy, he'd also spent a year at the U.S. Naval Academy Preparatory

School in Newport, Rhode Island, where he lived under a version of the Honor Concept.

THE HONOR CONCEPT OF THE UNITED STATES NAVAL ACADEMY

Midshipmen are persons of integrity: WE STAND FOR THAT WHICH IS RIGHT.

We tell the truth and ensure that the full truth is known: WE DO NOT LIE.

We embrace fairness in all actions. We ensure that work submitted as our own is our own, and that assistance received from any source is authorized and properly documented: WE DO NOT CHEAT.

We respect the property of others and ensure that others are able to benefit from the use of their own property: WE DO NOT STEAL.

I found it odd that Adrain wanted to meet with me for extra instruction (EI) so early in the semester, especially when he had an A in our course. This grand pronouncement was obviously on his mind because he couldn't wait to blurt it out to me when he arrived in our classroom right after school and before he headed off to boxing practice, where he prepared to defend his Brigade boxing championship he won as a Plebe (freshman).

"Why now? Why do you suddenly get it?"

Adrain explained what Gen Z would call his "deep story." He never knew his mother, who struggled significantly with substance abuse, and his father had challenges of his own, raising three kids on a custodian's salary. Food was not plentiful, and if it was, it was usually not the most nutritious. Physical moves were common, often one step in front of an irate landlord. Adrain described how it was commonplace to come home from school only to find that the electricity was off due to a delinquent bill, as well as the apartment's water. Oftentimes, a shower after school was out of a pail of water.

Fortunately, the first mentor in his life emerged while he was in high school, and he saw in Adrain what I saw: a smart, hardworking, dynamic young man who was fighting an uphill battle in life and needed guidance that wasn't available to him at home, where sheer survival ruled the day. This mentor introduced him to the Naval Academy, and with a lot of help and luck, Adrain was admitted to the Naval Academy Preparatory School. He certainly didn't crush it, but somehow, some way, he did enough to squeak into the Naval Academy. However, without a major course correction in his life—based on his current skill set—he had virtually no chance of graduating and commissioning into the Navy or Marine Corps.

I was a little taken aback by Adrain's candor. We had only been in class for a month, yet he unburdened himself of lots of emotional baggage. *What did I do to unleash this spigot of personal history?* I wondered.

"You explained honor in a way that finally made sense to me. Previously, it didn't connect with me that as midshipmen, we were called to a higher standard, and that standard was not of our choosing; the standard was the standard. I was born in the inner city, I was truly a child of the street, and I grew up viewing right and wrong in a very different way: Right is what you get away with, and wrong is when you get caught."

"The time we've spent together in class has shown me that that simply isn't the case. Midshipmen, by virtue of being midshipmen, do not lie, cheat, or steal. When you discussed this in class the other day, I finally realized this and now understand I haven't been living up to this ideal."

As mentors, we never know when we'll be presented with a chance to truly influence and, hopefully, change the trajectory of someone's life. At that moment, I knew such an opportunity was upon me. *How do I connect with a young black male with a personal history so different from my own?* The answer was, I had to meet him where he was, not where I was, nor where I thought he should be (after almost three years in the USNA system)—but where he *was!*

As our conversation continued, I learned (not surprisingly) that Adrain's Naval Academy journey was not going smoothly; quite the contrary, he was failing in most aspects of midshipman life. The previous fall, he cheated—and was caught—on his physics final, and now faced an honor board. His rationale at the time was quite simple: he was failing the class anyway, so he had nothing to lose by cheating. Pragmatic, yes. Honorable, no. His grades were well below the minimum GPA of 2.0, and he was subject to an academic review board to ascertain whether he could complete the curriculum at USNA.

Wow, this kid has issues and is going to require a lot of time and effort. With all his areas of struggle, where do I begin?

THE STRATEGY

MEET THE MENTEE WHERE THEY ARE

As a mentor, meeting your mentee where they are is critical to establishing and building rapport, crucial to success in the mentoring relationship. It wouldn't be productive to chastise Adrain for his many errors; he was acutely aware of his difficulties. As a mentor, it wouldn't be helpful for me to point out the obvious. Nor would it be constructive to recount a story of my time at the Naval Academy, beginning with the eye-rolling, "When I was a mid." No, wherever Adrain was, that's where I needed to be.

IDENTIFY STRENGTHS IN AREAS THEY'RE PASSIONATE ABOUT

A crucial piece of meeting a mentee where they are is to find an area in their life where they are having success. It may not be readily apparent, and this is why rapport is so important. A question like, "What's an accomplishment that you are really proud of?" is a great way to identify positive traits or skills that have proven helpful in other areas of their life and then pivot it to the area(s) where they are struggling.

In Adrain's case, rather than focusing on his academic difficulties, of which there were many, and realizing that his fundamental understanding of right and wrong ("get away with" versus "caught") was shaped by his challenging upbringing, I focused on something that *was* working for him. In Adrain's case, it was boxing.

The Naval Academy is one of the few universities in the country with a varsity boxing program and Adrain, as a freshman, won the Academy's championship in his weight class. Certainly, training to be a champion boxer took hard work, practice, and discipline—the exact same qualities to be successful in the classroom. Was there a way to connect the two?

The first thing we did was identify the skill sets that made him a boxing champion and translate them into academics.

Proverbs 27:17 (NIV), "As iron sharpens iron, one person sharpens another," applies to many life circumstances. The Naval Academy's boxing team was no exception. If you don't surround yourself with other good boxers, it's difficult to get better, no matter how much you train and spar. Adrain's boxing coaches understood this and did a superb job of continually testing their boxers against one another to sharpen them.

On the contrary, Adrain's roommates and "friend group" were in just as bad a shape academically as he was; no iron sharpened the other iron in his dorm room. So, when room assignments for the following fall opened, he got into a room with two serious students who provided a stable environment where study time was truly study time.

APPLY THEIR STRENGTHS IN AREAS THEY CHOOSE TO IMPROVE

To be successful in any athletic endeavor, you must have access to good coaching. That applies to life as well; most successful people in any field have coaches. However, a coach is only effective if the person being coached is "coachable", i.e., checks their ego, is open to suggestions, and willing to implement those suggestions.

Adrain had excellent, long-tenured boxing coaches who not only knew proper boxing procedures but were able to communicate those techniques to their athletes effectively. Together, we realized that to be successful academically, he needed to get academic "coaching," whether through extra instruction, midshipman-led tutoring sessions, or help from the academic center. A good athlete knows where they need help, asks their coach for it, and is "coachable". Adrain needed to do the same with his professors.

There are other examples, but holistically, by focusing on the one area where he was successful (boxing) and using it as an analogy for "getting his game together" in other areas of his life, Adrain was able to rise above his inauspicious beginnings and began to not only survive the Naval Academy, but to thrive.

USE REAL-WORLD EXAMPLES

Meeting your mentee where they are is galvanized when real-world examples are used. Using real-life examples not only helps the mentee understand the concept you are trying to get across, but by putting it in an example that directly relates to their past experiences, shows the mentee that you "get them".

As an Adjunct Professor at the Naval Academy, I teach a course (NE203) entitled Ethics and Moral Reasoning for the Naval Leader. The course is team-taught, and I'm charged with taking the academic portion taught by a civilian professor and translating that into real-world examples future young naval officers can use when they get to the fleet.

The course consists of four blocks; the first is Moral Perception. During this block of instruction, we consider how we perceive the moral world and factors that may bias or interfere with that perception. Our first reading is Christian Smith's 2003 article *Living Narratives,* and we use Smith's article to discuss cultural narratives.

USING CULTURAL NARRATIVES TO CONNECT WITH YOUR MENTEE

As a mentor, regardless of the wisdom we have and are willing to impart, if we're not able to connect or relate in a meaningful way, our mentoring won't be effective. Think of it like speaking the same language. I can have great knowledge and a lot of answers, but if I can only communicate in French to a Spanish speaker, it simply won't matter. This is where the idea of cultural narratives comes in.

What is a cultural narrative? Cultural narratives are the story of our community, telling us who we are as a community and how we ought to live our lives, i.e., our own personal deep stories. The salient point I make in my classroom is that we all have our own cultural narratives (deep stories). If we're going to lead our people effectively, we need to understand their cultural narratives and realize theirs may be wildly different from our own. However, ours is not better than theirs; it's just different.

The same applies to mentoring. If you're going to meet them where they are, you must know where they are, how they grew up, what values they learned, how they were raised, what's important to them, what they like, what they don't like, etc. Note: this information may be wildly different from your answers to those same questions!

We can't meet them where they are unless we know where they are. So, before we begin tactical-level mentoring, we must get to know them, find out where they are, and go to them.

What happened with Adrain, you might ask? Well, he did not finish strong in my class. His early semester success quickly vanished, and with a resounding F on the final exam, he ended up with a C in the course. However, there was light at the end of the tunnel. Adrain's grades stabilized a bit that semester (no doubt at the expense of NE 203), and while he continued to struggle with academics until his senior year, he was on an upward trajectory and trending toward graduating.

Once his academics smoothed out, Adrain was able to spend more time on the military side of academy life and started to receive billets (positions) that allowed his leadership skills to shine. He held a significant leadership role during the first semester of his senior year and capped it off by serving as the company commander of his company in the second semester, the senior midshipman among his 150+ peers. This incredible and improbable journey culminated with him receiving his commission as a Second Lieutenant in the United States Marine Corps, where he is currently a logistics officer for a Marine Aircraft Group. He also won two more Naval Academy boxing titles and two national titles before graduating.

James R. McNeal is a 1986 graduate of the United States Naval Academy and retired Rear Admiral. He is now semi-retired, enjoying doing whatever the heck he wants to do. This includes working as an Adjunct Professor at the United States Naval Academy, coaching football at St Mary's High School in Annapolis, Maryland, and mentoring with the Severn Leadership Group.

This is his fourth book; he has three previous titles: *The Herndon Climb*, *Side by Side in Eternity*, and *Crucibles*.

He and his wife Peggy, also a 1986 USNA grad, have been married for 37 years, have three adult children, and four grandchildren, with another on the way.

Connect with James:

LinkedIn: https://www.linkedin.com/in/james-mcneal-4a9977/

The Herndon Climb: https://bit.ly/4ojowLU

Side by Side in Eternity: https://amzn.to/3HfP8N1

Crucibles: http://bit.ly/4oebbVf

References

Smith, Christian. "Living Narratives." Moral, Believing Animals, July 10, 2003, 63–94. https://doi.org/10.1093/acprof:oso/9780195162028.003.0004

United States Naval Academy. "Honor Concept." Accessed June 26, 2025. https://www.usna.edu/About/honorconcept.php

CHAPTER TWELVE

BRIDGING THE GAP

MENTORING A MUSLIM
FROM THE HINDU CULTURE

David J. Foster, MBA, CPA

Mentoring across cultures is critical to unlocking the potential of multicultural international organizations. Given the multicultural makeup of many countries today, it's also key for companies in our home country.

MY STORY

My mentee, Ibrahim Kahn, faced a career-changing decision. Would he stick with the technical expertise he had worked so hard to obtain? Or would he take on team leadership that would open new possibilities for his future? While I knew we needed his leadership, I had listened carefully to his story in previous sessions and was dedicated to unconditional support for him, whatever he decided.

As the senior vice president of the automation business at a major multinational, I was tasked with presenting an opportunity to Ibrahim.

Would he continue as a leading technologist or shift to leading our Singapore engineering team? How could I support him through his decision?

Because people are so critical in our automation business, I often met with front-line engineers for counseling reviews about their careers in every one of the 35 countries where we had operations. We shared our passion for automation technologies and the values of our company: integrity, communication, problem-solving, and independent thinking, but we often came from very different cultures and held different faiths. As an American Christian, how could I build rapport with and support people like Ibrahim, a Muslim from India's Hindu culture? Ibrahim was the worldwide expert on our Distributed Control System ("DCS"). I found him talking with a small team of engineers among the equipment cabinets. After he concluded, we headed out for lunch.

Across the street, there was a row of small food trucks. At a noodle truck, we chose a delicious broth and a kind lady dropped noodles in our bowls, adding fresh spices and cold drinks. The equatorial sun was overhead, but a breeze off the sea moderated the temperature.

We found a small table and a couple of chairs. After catching up on events since my last trip to Singapore, I moved to the issue at hand. "Ibrahim, George is retiring as manager of our engineering team here and returning to the UK."

"Yes, and we'll miss him. All of us like and respect George," Ibrahim said.

"I've talked to the president of our Singapore company, and we'd like you to consider replacing George and managing the engineering team here."

Ibrahim went silent. I could see he was surprised and considering his response. I asked, "Well, what are you thinking?"

"David, I'm honored by this offer. However, you know that I love problem-solving within our DCS projects. Why would I leave that to become a manager?"

Ibrahim trusted me with the key question of his upcoming decision. Now, I had to honor his trust with my best response.

"That's the key question, Ibrahim. Like you, I love working on technology problems in our business. In my role, I continue to collaborate with our top talent, including you, on complex technical issues, while also facing the challenges that come with developing and leading teams worldwide.

"I've watched you lead others in your role as an expert. You have real abilities in communications and leadership. The question is, do you want to add more people challenges to your life as the manager of the engineering team? Working with people is at least as interesting as working with technology."

Ibrahim tracked my words. "You're asking if I want to add a new dimension to my work?"

"Well, I think you'll be growing a dimension you already experience, Ibrahim. I do want you to know I'll continue to support you in any way I can, whatever you decide."

"How long do I have to decide?"

"We want to announce George's replacement before he leaves next month. I hope you can work through this before I leave in three days. We see you as the best candidate for this job, Ibrahim, and will give you the time you need."

"Thank you, David. I'll talk this over with my wife and let you know my response before you leave."

"Great. If your wife has questions for me, I would love to have dinner with you both tomorrow evening. You know I'll be available to you any time in the coming days to talk through your decision making."

As we parted, I could see that Ibrahim was already deep in thought on the opportunity I had offered him. Our conversation had moved quickly and honestly to the key issues. And Ibrahim knew he could count on my support whichever way he decided.

How did we get to that point? And how did I prepare for this moment with my Muslim friend from the middle of India?

MENTORING ACROSS CULTURES

Earlier in my career, I was promoted to the management team of AccuRay Corporation, a worldwide automation company of 2,000 people. The CEO and COO were older than the rest of the team. The COO mentored each of us through our careers. We realized we should emulate the mentoring that had meant so much to us, so we developed and implemented a corporate program called Counseling Reviews.

At least annually, each associate met with their boss's boss to discuss their career. For me, this meant mentoring hundreds of engineers over the coming years. Turnover, a huge cost for any company dedicated to training and developing its people, dropped to half the previous rate! And it stayed there through the following years. Needless to say, I retained this program through the two mergers. I first met and mentored Ibrahim in this program.

Ibrahim decided to add the people puzzle to technological puzzles in his role and became the manager of our Singapore engineering team. As expected, he excelled in leading this group of Chinese, Malaysian, Indonesian, and American engineers. He later became the manager of our largest R&D group in Europe, the Managing Director of our Indian subsidiary with 10,000 employees, and finally joined the company's executive committee as Chief Technical Officer.

Other distinguished cross-cultural mentees of mine included:

- A Hindu Indian who became the president of the US. subsidiary of over 20,000 people, then joined the executive committee. He left the company to become CEO of a Fortune 500 company in the US.

- A newly hired French-Canadian engineer who became the vice president and general manager of a major automation company in Canada. She was then promoted to president of their worldwide automation operations.

I played a role in the development of these star performers, but I also played a role in developing hundreds of careers in locations worldwide. Let's turn now to the strategies that will equip you to have this kind of impact on your teams. Mentoring with cultural awareness, listening, and unconditional support will help you bridge the cultural gap.

THE STRATEGY

MASTER MENTORING

A fundamental discovery over a lifetime of building relationships and businesses in every inhabited continent is this: Beneath our cultural and religious differences, we humans are much more similar than we are different. The virtues on which this book is based—love, integrity, truth, excellence, and relationships practiced with courage—are highly regarded everywhere. As we practice mentoring as described in the chapters of this book, we learn to mentor across any difference in culture or faith. What follows are practices to emphasize, and some particular guidance for, mentoring through those differences.

CULTURAL AWARENESS

Cultural awareness starts with the simple knowledge that you're going into a different culture. Preparation by reading about that culture, its history, or keeping up with the culture's news is also helpful, but such preparation does not make an expert. Despite preparation, make no assumptions about how the culture works in a mentoring (or any) relationship.

Be certain to ask others about your new mentee. Supervisors and coworkers can often help prepare for a first meeting in ways appropriate to their culture.

Finally, don't fear raising the issue in a new relationship by being forthright, saying, "I'm new to your culture, so please let me know if I'm saying or doing anything offensive to you." Enlist your mentee as a guide to their culture. Propose agreements to address any unease either may feel, and to establish a safe place in your time together.

In Ibrahim's case, having worked in Bangalore, India, I knew a bit about the Hindu culture. I knew that Kahn was a Muslim name, and that many Muslims had left India to form Pakistan, but I knew nothing about how that history applied to his life.

LISTEN!

Listening is a key skill for any mentor, but it's even more effective when encountering another culture. Listen first and often in a different culture. In early meetings, ask your mentee to tell you about their life story. Listen carefully and ask questions to clarify understanding and to propel the story further and deeper. Ask about feelings that may have arisen in situations they describe.

In response to such a question early in our relationship, Ibrahim told me of his grandfather taking him to villages he owned during a time of Indian land reform. In each village, a line formed, and his grandfather gave the head of each family a deed to the land they'd worked for generations. To each of them, his grandfather said, "This is the deed to your land, but remember it actually belongs to my grandson, Ibrahim."

From this story, I knew that Ibrahim came from a powerful family. From the way he told the story, I also understood that he felt no such claim to the farmers' lands, and was glad to have moved on into a high-tech career in the States, and then in Singapore. Much of Ibrahim's relaxed social presence came from his intellect and expertise, but I also understood it came from his family background.

UNCONDITIONAL SUPPORT

A mentor must focus on the needs, desires, and vision of the mentee. While we may bring more knowledge and experience to the relationship, our purpose is to provide support, not to impose our will or to place the needs of the organization above those of the mentee.

When I promised to support Ibrahim in whatever he decided, I was dead serious! While I thought becoming a manager would be good for Ibrahim and our company, I valued Ibrahim himself, his desires, and his decision above all else. I learned this when mentees shared they were considering leaving our company. The knee-jerk reaction to such a revelation is to convince a valued employee to stay on and remain in the company. But I found this approach to be impractical, destructive to our relationship, and counter to my integrity. Of course, I honestly told them the advantages of building their career in the company where their record and reputation were highly valued, but I made it clear in every case that my principal concern was to support them in their decision.

DIFFERENT FAITHS

The history of religious faith is often a key factor in culture. Many people accept this aspect of their Christian, Muslim, Hindu, Buddhist, Shinto, or other cultures, whether they invest it with their belief or not. As a cultural and believing Christian, I see everyone I meet as an image of God, but I regard any effort on my part to push my faith into a mentoring conversation as a violation of the trust that is so important to a relationship.

I've found mentee inquiries on faith to be infrequent and often motivated by curiosity. So, honest, straightforward answers are appropriate and appreciated. When the conversation moves on, I let my mentee's interest be my guide. As often happens in mentoring relationships, Ibrahim became a good friend, and to my knowledge, he continues to practice his family's Muslim faith.

BRIDGING THE GAP THROUGH CHANGE

I have found two actions that support people through change. The first is a personal presentation by the responsible leader as soon as possible, describing the issues driving change and the possible outcomes. The second is mentoring by that leader for each of the individuals involved in the change. Here is one example of this approach.

At AccuRay, most of our finance operations were in our Columbus headquarters. However, we set up a finance department of 15 people in Brussels to meet local requirements in each European subsidiary and to support the country managers.

With growth, we reached a point where we had to decide whether to continue with this model or develop finance functions separately in each country, thereby eliminating the European finance department in Brussels.

First, we had a meeting with our Brussels finance people. I described our need to find the best solution for finance in Europe, asked for their support, and promised they would be the first to know our conclusions. I then asked each of them to meet with me over the coming days to understand their situation and answer any questions they might have. Before I left, I let them know I would be back every month and would be available for further mentoring sessions upon request.

After three months of gathering information, it was clear that the time had come to shut down the European Finance group in Brussels and build up appropriate finance support in each country. But we'd need the support of the Brussels team through a transition that would last around 12 months.

At another meeting of the whole group, I explained our decision and our rationale. I asked for their continued professional support through the transition. Belgian law gave each of them a required notice period before termination of employment. These ranged from six to 24 months, depending on the individual's age and time with the company. If they stayed with us through the transition and kept a positive attitude, they would receive their notice period as a severance with no requirement to work. If they soured and complained to their coworkers, the notice of termination would take effect immediately. Once again, I met with every employee to hear their concerns and answer their questions.

Twelve months later, the transition came to a successful end. We had terminated only one employee who became negative several months into the transition. The rest performed their work with professionalism and a positive attitude. I attended a goodbye party for all the finance personnel who were leaving. At this party, every member of the team took me aside to say thanks. Each said they felt heard and respected. Each had a positive story to tell about how they had leveraged their known severance benefit to improve their life.

Two of the women were pregnant, using the severance pay to allow time off to have and care for their babies. Several used their severance to buy a house. Another planned to start a new business. Coming up with a creative Belgian solution and mentoring each Belgian team member before, during, and after the decision were key factors in managing a very difficult change.

CONCLUSION

I understand apprehension around mentoring someone from another culture, but it's clear to me that despite the importance of cultural behaviors and beliefs, our shared humanity means mentoring works across cultures.

Most importantly, you can do it! If you master mentoring as we describe it in this book and observe these strategies with courage, you can make a big difference for each of your business associates from other cultures and beyond, into other aspects of your life. Preparing cultural awareness, practicing deep listening, offering unconditional support, and respecting other faiths are the paths to take when mentoring outside your own culture, and I promise you will share the joy it has brought me!

David Foster is an SLG Mentor who has developed and led large, international, high-tech organizations.

David has experienced exceptional mentoring throughout his life. His parents, Jack and Julie Foster, raised him with love, integrity, and a strong Christian faith. Ed Kelly, the superintendent of a manufacturing plant, showed him how to lead working people. Football coaches Joe Venturi and Carm Cozza taught him the power of teamwork and servant leadership.

After earning an engineering degree at Yale, David married Joanne and earned an MBA at Harvard Business School. He then became a U.S. Navy Supply Corps officer.

Supply Corps Commander Ted Walker mentored him on how to lead in and navigate the politics of the Navy. Chris Campbell, COO of AccuRay Corporation in Columbus, Ohio, mentored him through 20 years of growth from department head to VP of Sales and Service in Europe and Chief Financial Officer. He then showed him how to survive and prosper through mergers into Combustion Engineering and ABB.

Inspired by Chris Campbell's mentoring, David and AccuRay's management team created a program in which every associate reviewed their careers with their boss's boss. This mentoring halved turnover and accelerated the development of the engineering resource.

As Senior VP of ABB Automation Service in Zurich, he led over 2,500 people in this business, more than doubling its revenues and increasing profits from five percent to 20%. He mentored people in 35 countries, including a Chinese leader who started the first wholly owned foreign entity in China.

Now, David mentors ex-prisoners re-entering society, SLG Fellows, and others. He loves and mentors his family, especially his eight grandchildren. Joanne and David enjoy getting away to sail their boat on Lake Erie every summer.

Connect with David:

LinkedIn: https://www.linkedin.com/in/david-foster-6b85b646/

Email: djfoste7@icloud.com

PART: 4

ADVANCED TECHNIQUES

CHAPTER THIRTEEN

SO, WHAT'S THE PROBLEM?

GETTING TO THE HEART OF THE MATTER

Judy Farrell, MAAL, CPC

MY STORY

I'm totally going to fail! Breathe. Why can't I think?

"I just really need to get these files downloaded," my client says, "but I don't know what I'm doing, and every time I try, I just stare at the computer screen."

Ugh! This isn't the type of struggle I plan to help with. I don't want to work with people freaking out about technology issues.

Rolling my eyes, I take a breath, willing anything intelligent to repopulate my now-empty brain.

Okay, focus on the call. What did she just say?

"What have you tried so far?"

Good open-ended question. Wait, am I supposed to be into problem-solving this early in the conversation? Darn it, she stopped talking. What did she say? I forgot to listen!

"Tell me more."

Good save. Oh, wait. That response didn't make sense. Why is this so hard? I thought I'd be good at this! Oh no. She stopped talking again.

"Is there anyone who could sit with you to help?"

Ugh! That was a closed-ended question. Also, I'm giving advice in the form of a question. What am I supposed to say?!

I've always had an innate sensitivity: a natural gift of understanding what someone else is feeling. It equipped me with the ability not to judge others. I can understand where they're coming from, even when I don't agree with their line of thinking, conclusion, or behavior. It took me a while to figure out what went wrong in my first coaching evaluation for my professional coaching certification. Then it hit me.

That annoyance I felt was *judgment* in disguise!

What?! I don't judge people! It's kinda my thing! I'm not a judger!

Yep. Totally judging. And it was distracting both of us from understanding the *actual* struggle my client faced and getting to the heart of the matter.

It was distracting me because I could not relate to her struggle and became annoyed, rather than curious. I had automatically deemed the struggle as ridiculous because I could not relate to it. I have never struggled downloading files on a computer. This didn't seem like a "real" problem worthy of my time.

It was distracting her because she also couldn't understand why such a "simple" task was so hard for her to tackle. As a successful professional, she *should* be able to handle this. It was embarrassing. She was judging herself.

Ultimately, I didn't completely fail because this scenario was just the first practice coaching session with a master coach pretending to be a client. However, it was incredibly humbling, and I learned A LOT, to say the least!

So, what does this have to do with mentoring? I'm glad you asked. In a word: everything.

Although coaching and mentoring are different, there's a lot of overlap. For one, they share a similar desire to help others grow and succeed. They also both, as I quickly learned, require a great deal of humility. As a coach or a mentor, you must learn to practice what you teach, be open to new experiences and learn new skills, and become much more self-aware.

Sometimes what you learn about yourself through the process, however, can be disconcerting! For me, it was learning that I am clearly not as empathetic and humble as I had thought. Ouch!

However, the most important similarity between coaching and mentoring is the ability to listen deeply. There are a couple of skills you can learn to help keep you focused when your mentee brings up a topic you're not sure how to address, or your lack of understanding distracts you from getting to the heart of the matter.

THE STRATEGY

As much as we want to believe we're rational beings, the truth is, our hearts (emotions) guide us. I mention getting to the "heart" of the matter because our struggles are often emotional, not logical. Luckily, the following skills can help prevent you from wasting time trying to solve the wrong issue.

SKILL ONE: ACKNOWLEDGING

Acknowledging leads to *your* understanding because you must listen well enough to repeat back what you understand. Understanding frees *you* from judgment because when you fully understand the situation, it will make sense as to what's leading to your mentee's struggle. Often, what we may initially deem a character flaw or moral failing, we discover is a lack of skill, knowledge, or experience.

The trickiest part—the part that takes a lot of practice—is listening for emotion, particularly when they don't explicitly state it. Not everyone is good at expressing or even being aware of what they are feeling. Unfortunately, a lack of awareness doesn't prevent anyone from being heavily influenced by emotion. You're more likely to be controlled by emotions if you're unaware of or ignoring them.

Some people are excellent at expressing their feelings. If someone tells you what they're feeling, fantastic! You can mirror that back to them in the form of a question to ensure you understand correctly.

"So, when X happens, you feel Y?" or "You're feeling Y because X happened?"

On the other hand, someone may not tell you directly how they're feeling, like in my botched coaching session. In this case, you'll need to employ empathy and observe body language to decipher their feelings.

Instead of jumping straight to trying to solve the "problem," I wish I'd stated, "Wow, it sounds like trying to figure out how to download these files is causing a lot of anxiety." I could have then stayed quiet to allow her to confirm or correct my understanding of the situation, or ask if I understood her correctly.

I could have also encouraged her to tell me more if I didn't glean what she was feeling from her initial explanation of the problem. As the conversation continued, I learned she was anxious about downloading the files because she had made a mistake in the past that wiped her entire computer.

Well, that made so much more sense to me! I've felt anxious before. It caused my mind to go blank. It had just happened in real time!

Being able to resonate with the experience of being anxious set me up to employ the second skill needed.

SKILL TWO: VALIDATION

Validating someone's feelings can only happen if you understand *why* they're feeling that emotion in the first place. When you validate that their feelings are normal given their circumstances, they'll stop judging themselves for feeling as they do, which will free their mind to focus on problem-solving.

Validation is quite simple. Think of all the different ways you can say, "Of course you feel X, given that Y happened!" or "Anyone might feel X if they experienced Y as you did!"

The key is recognizing how they felt, not how you might have felt, in that situation. Focusing on how you may have experienced a scenario rather than on how someone else did is an aspect of empathy many get wrong. When you try to put yourself in someone else's "shoes," you may inadvertently take yourself (your experiences, skills, values, beliefs, etc.) with you. In other words, you try to walk around in *their world* while still wearing *your shoes.*

My client's struggle wasn't her inability to download files. If that had been the case, she wouldn't have needed coaching; she would have needed to chat with someone in technology. The "shoes" I needed to put on were ones of extreme anxiety.

"Of course, your mind went blank when you tried downloading the files! Who wouldn't get anxious after accidentally wiping their computer?"

Why does this work? Because we often *judge ourselves* for feeling how we're feeling. We believe we're overreacting, which causes us to feel inadequate. If we feel incapable in a situation, we lose faith in our ability to overcome the obstacle.

By validating, or normalizing, what someone is feeling, you let them know they can feel what they feel (because it is "normal" to feel that way) while also pushing through the feeling to achieve their goal. In other words, what they feel is real, but their conclusion about what that feeling says about them is likely inaccurate. That is to say, just because they feel inadequate doesn't mean they are.

TROUBLESHOOTING

The hardest part of learning to acknowledge and validate is the awkwardness of learning how to do it. If you try to follow a formula, it feels (and will come across as) inauthentic. You might need to follow the example formulas I mentioned at first, but you will want to practice enough that it flows naturally. Trying to follow a formula will distract you, as you'll be so busy trying to come up with the "correct" response instead of listening.

However, I hate to break it to you, but there's no getting around the awkwardness as you learn and practice.

Just as you'll encourage others to push through uncomfortable feelings as you mentor them, I'm encouraging you to recognize your discomfort and forge ahead. Having the courage to do so now will allow you to lend that courage to others as you mentor them in the future.

I'm convinced that these skills will help all your relationships, not just in mentoring.

My husband had the opportunity to learn these skills when he went to a three-day coaching workshop at Georgetown University. He has a tell when he's feeling awkward or uncomfortable. After years of marriage, I can spot his discomfort a mile away. Not only was it already awkward for him to practice these skills, but add to the mix he was trying something new in front of his wife, whose opinion of him matters a lot. She's also a certified coach, so these skills are *her* specialty! Talk about pressure!

And yet, he persisted over and over. One day, I was struggling with a problem, and he acknowledged and validated that struggle. The fog lifted, and I could see the solution as clear as day!

He got to be my hero that day because he leaned into the discomfort of learning something new until these skills were no longer a formula. They became so natural, he hadn't realized he'd used them.

Please don't underestimate the power of these skills or shy away because they're difficult or unnatural at first. Impacting the lives of others takes courage.

Here are a few other ways you may catch yourself in the judging trap I found myself in:

- You catch yourself saying something like, "Well, if I were you…" (giving advice)
- You think they may be overreacting
- You feel annoyed or impatient

If you find yourself in any of these situations, remember you can combat it by taking another step toward a deeper understanding of the problem. With that said, I'm not saying you aren't justified in finding yourself in any of the situations above. I'm saying they may be signs you don't fully understand the problem, particularly if the situation develops early in the conversation.

Advice-Giving: You want to delay this for as long as possible. It's so gratifying to give others advice that this, too, will take practice. You should delay because allowing others to come up with their solution empowers them on many levels. I'll share only three:

1. Delaying your advice facilitates critical thinking.
2. It increases confidence through achievement.
3. It enables them to take ownership of the solution, increasing their chance of successful implementation.

What to do instead: Even if your mentee asks for advice, you can delay giving it by asking them what advice they'd give to someone else in their situation. Then, discuss how they might be able to implement their advice.

Judgment: Again, if you catch yourself judging, you likely don't fully understand the context of the situation.

What to do instead: "Tell me more" is my go-to prompt when I get stuck. Just keep in mind there are a few situations in which this phrase won't make sense!

Impatience: This can be a sign of judgment. It can also be a sign your mentee is stuck. If your impatience stems from their repeated struggle with the same issue, try to get curious about it.

What to do instead: Point out that the two of you have discussed this struggle, or something similar, before. Ask your mentee what brought them back to it. Was their previous solution not implemented? Did it not work? What can you learn from their attempt, or lack thereof, to make adjustments?

THE ANTIDOTE TO JUDGMENT

Okay, I know that was a lot! The bottom line is that judging can sneak into your mentoring and sabotage your efforts. Even if you're not judging, your mentee might be judging themselves, which can also hinder their efforts to find an actionable solution. The antidote to judging is understanding.

For both of you to reach an understanding, you can acknowledge and validate. Using these tools will have the added benefit of taming big emotions, allowing for better problem-solving.

Finally, these skills take time and practice. More importantly, they require courage to learn. However, the payoff is the opportunity to be someone's hero. Go forth with courage and change lives!

Judy Farrell, MAAL, CPC, is the CEO of Judy Ann Farrell Coaching and co-owns and operates Acres Aweigh Farm Stay in New Glarus, Wisconsin, with her husband and three children. She's a speaker, author, and certified professional coach.

After six years of serving as a Surface Warfare Officer in the U.S. Navy, she spent another three years traveling the country, conducting leadership development courses for junior and senior naval officers as a Navy Reservist. During this time, she earned her M.A. in Administrative Leadership from the University of Oklahoma.

Judy has been training and developing leaders and mentors professionally for over 15 years. Her passion lies in serving those who serve others, which led her to Severn Leadership Group as a fellow, and then as the Director of Programs in 2019, where she spearheaded the revamp of the fellowship program and expansion of the mentor training program, as well as developed a training program for program managers.

Following a devastating medical crisis and her husband's retirement from the Navy, she and her family moved to Wisconsin to be near family and help others discover joy through connecting to good food, nature, and community on their farm. She would love to connect with you, either virtually through her website or in person on the farm. Head to either website to learn more about her professional services or how to visit the farm. Be sure to sign up for her newsletters, as she is generous with the resources she sends to her email subscribers. She looks forward to getting to know you!

Connect with Judy:

Professional Services
Website: https://JudyAnnFarell.com
LinkedIn: https://www.linkedin.com/in/judyannfarrell

The Farm
Website: https://AcresAweighFarmStay.com
Instagram: https://www.instagram.com/acresaweighfarmstay

CHAPTER FOURTEEN

THE POWER OF PATIENCE

HOW TO BE A GUIDE ON THE SIDE

Renee Sherwood

MY STORY

The branches in the Magic Forest glistened with moisture on a crisp autumn morning. Every climbable surface in the campus' wooded grove reflected the previous evening's storm in droplets of silvery condensation. My kindergartners' wide, bright eyes betrayed their emotions as we approached the forest, although their masks hid their true smiles.

"Can we go to the higher branches today?" They looked up longingly and bargained with me before I had time to assess the liability of the situation.

Are you joking? You're five years old, and that's too dangerous. It's too wet. Too high. Too risky. We need to return to the safety of our classroom before anyone gets hurt. Where are the iPads when you need them?

"Well, everything looks wet from last night. I don't think we can today."

You would have thought I cancelled Christmas from the looks in their eyes.

"Okay, we can play out here, but no climbing—and if you're above the ground, we go in immediately," I said impatiently, trying to get the experience over with as quickly and safely as possible.

It was October 2020, and everything was dangerous. Deep in the pandemic, I returned to the classroom after a dozen years away and was teaching kindergartners at a progressive school in Annapolis, Maryland. My daughter and son both relocated to new schools to attend as much in-person instruction as was allowed at the time. Everything felt unpredictable and scary.

To add to the environment of fear, my dad recently had his first of many seizures, indicating a cancerous brain tumor diagnosis. To say things felt out of control was the understatement of the year.

Like most experiences in my life when things felt out of control, I doubled down on controlling any situation I could. There was little room for patiently waiting to see how things might turn out; I controlled the heck out of the given circumstances. That day, it started with climbing trees.

Fine, they can climb a little bit, but here are the rules.

"Okay, you can climb, but no higher than a foot off the ground."

"Be careful."

"You have to start from this spot."

"Stand under a friend and spot them."

"One at a time."

This is ridiculous; let's just go inside.

My approach to keeping my students safe in the forest that day was the same approach I took to everything at that time in my life. No time for questions, I know best, no patience, and I'll tell you what to do and why to do it.

Control. Control. Control.

It spilled over inside the classroom, through setting up strict groups for center time, assigning activities instead of letting the kids choose, making seating charts, and forbidding them to play with sticks on the playground. Forget curiosity and questioning, which was the hallmark of the school's philosophy; we didn't have time for that! At the time, a certain degree of extra oversight was necessary because of the seemingly impending doom of the global pandemic, but there could have been more space for engagement, independence, and exploration with my students.

In juxtaposition to my obsessive need to keep these kids safe and in line, there was another teacher in the First School who had a completely different approach to my micromanaging tendencies and teacher-knows-best attitude. While I told my kids to over-sanitize their hands and not ingest the flour in the communal kitchen, she had them sample all the ingredients. I insisted flour wouldn't taste good on its own, and she let them sample and compare it to a pinch of sugar. While I herded my kids away from the apparent danger of the slippery branches, she stood nearby asking questions.

"What do you think?"

"Is it a good day for climbing?"

"I wonder...?"

"Do you have a plan?" She patiently questioned and waited for them to think it through.

Instead of telling them what to do in every situation, she modeled curiosity and, ultimately, the patience to explore and arrive at the answers themselves. Instead of telling them flour was bland and dry by itself, she took the time to give each child a pinch and let them figure it out. Instead of sharing all the perils of climbing trees with wet branches and micromanaging their experience, she asked questions about how they planned to navigate the space. Instead of forbidding outdoor play on a rainy day, she exuded patience in letting the children put on their gear with minimal assistance and go outside to jump in the puddles. Instead of controlling them, she patiently gave them the room to grow.

At first, this approach appalled the controlling part of me. *These kids are going to get hurt, make bad decisions, fail, and God forbid, they may even go outside and get wet—or even worse, muddy, and I don't have the patience for that!* But as I stood back and watched her let her students arrive at the answers themselves throughout the day, I began to realize the value of this approach—the power of patience.

Practicing some patience and allowing students to arrive at their own conclusions made their discoveries meaningful to them. Instead of being told by an adult not to eat the flour because it tasted bad, the kids knew firsthand that it was the foundation for their sweet creations. A little pinch of something extra was all that was needed to enhance the flavor and make it their own.

The same happened on the playground and in the forest. If the students knew to pause and think through the situation they faced and received the trust to make their own decisions, they could navigate the outdoors confidently. If they had the space to discover an effective approach, then it stuck with them and became their own solution. They learned where to hold onto a branch or find a foothold through their own experience instead of what an adult had dictated to them.

I began to wonder: If this worked with preschoolers and kindergartners, how would this approach of infusing patience into my role as "teacher" impact my kids and other relationships? *What if I tried this in other areas of my life?*

While this seemed to be an epiphany at school, the actual practice of it was difficult for me. I ultimately left the classroom after several long COVID years and had to test this theory in other parts of my life. Standing back and allowing my own kids to discover answers required me to let go of a certain amount of control as a parent, something I doubled down on during the pandemic.

I started small, with some catch phrases I thought would encourage autonomy and discovery instead of the nagging mom approach. Teenagers being a great audience for experimental parenting, I tried asking my daughter questions instead of making demands. It required a tremendous amount of patience to ask, "What do you think is getting in the way of…?" Fill in the blank: cleaning your room, doing your homework, putting away your laundry?

This sort of questioning invited conversation instead of immediate push back, and sometimes the room even got cleaned. When given the opportunity to arrive at answers themselves, even when I had a solution in mind, it resonated more deeply with my kids than giving them an ultimatum or a solution of how I would do it up front. This was out of my comfort zone at first, but as I began to practice, I saw the value of infusing more patience in my parenting and giving my kids the space to forge their own paths.

As I experimented with this approach, I reflected: Was there an actual strategy for patience? Do you simply wait and ask questions? And to be more patient, do you just wait longer for some magic to happen? Not exactly. There's a little more to it.

THE STRATEGY

If you truly want to embrace the power of patience, you need to get out of your own way. As I heard from a wise mentor, stop being a sage on the stage and become a guide on the side. Not only is that challenging as a teacher and mentor in your relationships, but it's particularly challenging in our fast-paced culture that glorifies instant gratification. Don't know the answer? Google it. Forgot to stop for paper towels or milk? Amazon to the rescue. We rarely have to wait for anything, and miss the rewards of being patient ourselves or allowing others the space to arrive at their own answers.

What does that look like in practice? How do you practice patience?

First, you have to get comfortable with letting go of the notion that you have all the answers in any given situation. You may have many answers—heck, you may even have most of them—but I guarantee you don't have them all. Letting go of that line of thinking allows you to open up space for the fact that someone else might actually find more value in their own learning than what you have to teach them, and that you may, in turn, learn something in the process.

Next, get curious. Ask questions. Lots of them. And then ask more questions. Why? In the interest of time, I'll tell you the answer—but in practice, questioning fosters deeper connections and collaboration. Asking instead of telling can be a more effective communication style because you begin to build trust and create space for shared understanding. Open-ended questions that promote reflection are highly effective in giving someone else the opportunity to come to their own conclusions. As the psychologist Carl Jung said, "The right question is already half the solution to a problem."

Finally, provide some scaffolding. As a teacher, I needed to give my students the space for discovery, but that didn't mean I completely left them stranded in the forest, watching from afar. According to Grand Canyon University's teaching blog, scaffolding in education speak is "an instructional method where a teacher provides temporary support to help students learn new concepts or skills." As the students become more proficient, the teacher gradually reduces their support until the students are self-sufficient. It's meant to be a crutch to assist students in being independent. How does this connect to practicing patience? Asking questions can be a form of scaffolding—and steering someone in a direction that leads to clearer solutions or deeper understanding.

Wondering what this looks like? Let's go back to the forest.

"Can we go to the higher branches today?"

It definitely stormed last night. This is so out of my comfort zone. Okay, deep breath, let go, and be patient.

"Let's take a walk around the big tree."

"How does the forest look different from the last time we were here?"

Obviously, it rained. Their observation skills are working today.

"What do you think our plan should be for climbing today?"

"Tell me more."

"Do you think the forest will look different if we come out later today?"

"What did it look like last time we were here?"

Wait for it. Wait for it.

"Great idea! I think if we climb this afternoon, the branches will be dry, and we can try those higher spots."

Giving my students the space to figure out that climbing in the afternoon would allow them to tackle the higher branches gave them ownership over the solution to our climbing dilemma. They learned to pause and assess the situation, just as I paused and allowed them to come up with a better, safer plan. I stepped out of the way to let them find their way to a decision that made sense, provided some scaffolding by asking questions that pointed them in a direction but didn't give them answers, and ultimately allowed them to climb to greater heights with the power of patience.

Renee Sherwood is the Director of Programs and Events for the Severn Leadership Group. As a career educator, she spent a dozen years in the classroom before falling in love with nonprofit work.

As an educator, Renee spent most of her professional career in the classroom and working with underserved students in the community. After graduating from Towson University with a Master of Arts in teaching, she began her teaching career in Baltimore City Schools. Her career includes leadership roles such as grade-level chair and student achievement coach in the Adams 12 School District in Broomfield, Colorado.

Renee continued to support students outside the classroom by launching a tutoring program for children reading below grade level and living in subsidized housing in the Annapolis area. She later went on to oversee educational programming and trained mentors to support high school students as the founding Executive Director of Charting Careers in Annapolis, Maryland.

Renee also supported education in the arts as a program lead for Creating Communities, a nonprofit dedicated to increasing access to the arts in Annapolis. She has been active in community events and involved in supporting the PTA at her children's schools by serving as a committee chair, ambassador, and volunteer.

In addition to her role as an educator, Renee also fulfills the role of mom to a 13- and 16-year-old and a very large labradoodle. She enjoys being outside with her family, skiing, yoga, reading, and cooking. Renee loves to travel and explore, and is still trying to decide whether her heart belongs to the beach or the mountains.

Connect with Renee:

LinkedIn: https://www.linkedin.com/in/renee-sherwood-322764176/

Facebook: https://www.facebook.com/renee.g.sherwood

Instagram: https://www.instagram.com/teamsherwood5/

CHAPTER FIFTEEN

FROM CHAOS TO CALM

POWER OF PAUSE:
LESSONS FROM A PARENT OF TRIPLETS

Caitríona Taylor, MBA

Have you ever felt so panicked that you don't know how you'll get through the next hour? Maybe you want to scream or run, but you can't do either. You just wish someone would walk in, say, "It'll be okay," and take over. If you want to learn how to get through those times, keep reading!

MY STORY

Is that smell poop, vomit, or both?

I'm sitting on my bed in the middle of the night.

My fingers search for the source of the smell. *Is it on me or all over the bed?*

My three newborns are screaming, each wanting to be held and fed. I wonder how long it's been.

Three hours?

I grab my phone and look at the clock.

It's 2:31 a.m. Only 21 minutes have passed. How did I get here?

Tonight, I slid into bed with three cribs around me—two on my right and one at the foot of the bed. I looked at my pregnancy pillow.

I won't need that tonight.

I was almost sad, thinking we wouldn't have our nightly meet-up, with all three tucked in at different angles as I fed them. They were getting into a rhythm, and I could feed one at a time. Gone were the days of propping bottles with my foot—I have triplets and only two hands—or so I thought.

That pillow supported me up to my thirty-second week of pregnancy. I even brought it to the hospital for my last week. It's a big, C-shaped pillow, longer than me, that I wrapped around myself as I struggled through pregnancy. I thought I'd be done with it already, but 12 weeks later, it still helped me. I could tuck one baby on their side and have a bottle nearby during night feeds.

The first six weeks after my babies were born, they were in the Neonatal Intensive Care Unit (NICU). The pillow was alone at home. I lost 48 pounds in ten days and didn't need it anymore. When my babies came home, they weighed just four and a half, four and a half, and five and a half pounds—so tiny the pillow would have swallowed them. That's why they only started using it at night a few weeks ago. We had many nights where all three were hungry at once. This pillow saved the day.

Tonight, I pushed the pillow aside. *Oh, how I'll miss these nights with just me and my three babies.* Most nights aren't easy, but I was happy after two good nights in a row. *We won't go backward!*

I snap back to reality as I hear my babies' shrieks. In those 21 minutes, all three woke up at once. I've already grabbed the bottles I prepared before bed and managed to warm them up. I decide the loudest baby gets the first bottle. As I feed one, I warm the next. I have two bottles in mouths and the third warming. I secure the first bottle on the pillow and get the third ready.

I sing my fifteenth verse of "Wheels on the Bus"—"The snakes on the bus go snakety snake snake"—but it doesn't soothe them. The bottles are empty, and the babies are still hungry. Their cries echo off each other.

Each baby cries for themselves and for their siblings. They want to know everything's okay. All are swaddled like burritos.

I look down at them. *Now would be a good time to have a partner.*

When I chose to take the leap as a single mother, I was understandably apprehensive. What would people think? How could I afford it? How would I handle it?

Never did I think I would be blessed with triplets. Sometimes I still Google the chances—less than one percent. *How was I to know? And how come I didn't realize this is what it would actually be like? What have I done?*

No time to think about that now. It's 2:42 a.m. and all the bottles are empty. As I scoop my hand under one baby, they feel slimy, and I realize the poop I smell is oozing out of their sleep sack. The baby next to them is covered in vomit. I only have one spare set of clothes and a sleep sack in the room, as I've never needed to swap out more than one during the night. All the formula and extra clothes are downstairs.

How am I to leave these screaming babies safely and get downstairs to get all the supplies?

Can someone please just come through that door and help me?!

But, the answer is yes; someone can come through that door and help me. That person is me.

I take a moment to assess what's going on. Clearly, my kids aren't going back to bed right now, as they're all still hungry and drank all the milk I had ready in the room.

I breathe in and exhale with intention to bring my awareness back into my body, repeating: *Inhale, exhale, inhale, exhale.*

I mentally figure out what I can control. I realize I'll have to leave everyone alone in the room so I can go get more food.

In that moment, the pause doesn't give me all the answers, but it gives me the space to breathe, to choose my next step, and to trust I can handle what comes next.

I struggle through the next 30 minutes. I put everyone safely back in their cribs, so no one chokes or gets hurt while I leave. I run downstairs to make formula, grab clothes, warm bottles, and run back upstairs. Babies still screaming, I start my routine again. Unswaddle, change diapers, change clothes, swaddle like burritos, prop on the pillow, safely feed them using my feet and hands to hold bottles as best I can. Keep singing "Wheels on the Bus."

Stay calm and take deep breaths. Keep my voice joyful and caring. Let them feel safe and secure. Be confident. Trust my ability to do this.

Finally, with the babies all fed and back to sleep, I go into the next room to pump. Adding my breastmilk to the formula helps, as it has antibodies and digests more easily. As I pump, I text myself how much everyone ate and at what time, so I make sure everyone eats enough throughout the day. I take half an hour to get what I can and bottle up to put in the ice bag. I slide back into the other room—4:45 a.m. I can get two and a half hours of sleep before I start this all over again.

It's nine a.m. and I'm sitting on my couch, looking at all three babies resting peacefully and safely in the swings across from me. I pause, taking a sip of my coffee, my hand shaking from the night's events.

I will never be unprepared again at night. I will never have a night like that again.

I review every detail of the night before and start to strategize about what I can do differently next time.

More spare formula in the room, made ahead of time. More extra sets of clothes, diapers, and supplies. Don't ever think you'll have an easy night ahead—always be prepared.

THE STRATEGY

As a new mentor, you may wonder, *Am I doing this right?* The truth is, there's rarely a perfect answer in the moment. The power of the pause is that it gives you a moment to assess, breathe, and control your actions with intention—even when you feel outnumbered by challenges, just as I did at 2:31 a.m. with three crying babies. Over time, these pauses build your courage and confidence. Each time you pause, you're not just surviving the moment—you're learning, growing, and becoming the leader your mentees need.

THE PAUSE: CREATING SPACE IN CHAOS

When you're in a moment of chaos, your fight-or-flight reaction can set in. It's normal for your brain to perceive a threat and trigger the release of hormones like adrenaline and cortisol. Your heart rate and blood pressure increase, your muscles tense, and you may even experience shaking or trembling. Think back to the moment I shared, surrounded by three screaming babies. I was unable to think past: *How did I get here?* And *can someone come save me?*

Think of a time when you felt overwhelmed as a mentor. What might have changed if you paused?

You can use the following ABC technique to harness the power of pause:

- **Assess the situation:** What is my mentee sharing with me right now, and why is this important to them?

- **Breathe with intention:** Focus on a steady inhale and exhale, while also actively listening to your mentee.

- **Control what you can control:** If you don't know what to say, ask clarifying reflection questions, such as, "What went well?" or, "What different outcome would you like?"

When you're in this moment, creating space can be hard, but it can also slow your thoughts and reactions, allowing you to make the best decision you can in that moment. Using the Multi-Health Systems model from Sig Berg's *The Virtue Proposition,* create this space in how you listen to and respond to your mentee. This can move you on to the decision-making building blocks:[1]

- Impulse control
- Reality testing
- Problem solving

---

1 Berg, Sig. The Virtue Proposition. Herndon: Amplify Publishing, 2024, 77.

IMPULSE CONTROL

When you first practice the power of pause, you may not be able to control all your reactions; the fight-or-flight response is sometimes just too strong. However, the opportunity with mentorship is that, as a mentor, you get to be that space where your mentee can go back to the moment to reflect on their actions, uncover the why behind their reaction, and determine what they could do differently if in a similar situation again. Your mentee isn't asking you to solve the difficult problem they're bringing forward. Instead, be that inviting cup of coffee in the morning. Sit with your mentee in the uncomfortable moments and guide them to explore what other options they could choose.

REALITY TESTING

One of the most valuable assets you bring to the mentor-mentee relationship is situational experience. Your mentee gets to tap into your wealth of knowledge and resources. As my three babies looked up at me, screaming with hunger, tiredness, and feeling uncomfortable in their diapers, they didn't know their current situation was temporary. If I responded using their understanding of the moment—screaming back and waiting for someone else to arrive with the much-needed food and clothing supplies—we would still be in that room. Instead, I applied my logic and skills to lift us all out of it. By attending to their basic needs (hunger, food, and sleep) and stretching myself out of my comfort zone, I restored harmony. Your mentee only knows their experience. Pausing for reflection and sharing appropriate experiences can help them understand that the reality they're currently experiencing may not be the only reality there is.

PROBLEM SOLVING

As a mentor, this is one of the hardest areas to avoid: solving your mentee's problem. It's really hard. One way for me to quiet all my babies right away would be to sedate them—problem solved! Now, yes, I'm being dramatic. I would never sedate my babies to sleep at night. But the analogy isn't far off. If you jump right to solving your mentee's problem—that is, removing the painful moment by telling them what to do—you are, in essence, "sedating" your mentee. Your role as a mentor is to cultivate the innate skills that lie within them. You must stretch your listening, reflecting, relationship, and trust-building skills to provide a space where your mentee feels safe to explore and grow. If you start to stumble and jump right into telling your mentee what to do, start back at your ABCs—assess, breathe, and control only what you can control!

PRACTICAL TAKEAWAYS FOR NEW MENTORS

- Practice the pause in stressful moments.
- Use the ABC technique: assess, breathe, control.
- After tough situations, debrief with yourself: What worked? What will you do differently next time?
- Seek feedback and share your experiences with other mentors. Remember, the learning curve is normal.

CONCLUSION: THE ENDURING POWER OF PAUSE

The power of pause is transformative—in parenting, mentoring, and leadership. Each pause is a chance to gather courage, reflect, and act with intention. As you grow in your mentoring journey, remember confidence is built one pause at a time. Trust yourself, embrace the unknown, and know you're exactly where you need to be for your mentees.

Caitríona Taylor, MBA, is a passionate advocate for mentorship and servant leadership. She has been an active mentor in the Severn Leadership Group (SLG) since 2020, guiding emerging leaders as they navigate new challenges and opportunities. Her leadership philosophy centers on fostering courage, confidence, and continuous growth in others.

With over 25 years of experience in leadership, health, and wellness, Caitríona is the Executive Director for Physical Education, Recreation, and Dance at Boston University and has held key leadership roles at MIT and Boston College. She has served as Executive Director for various state boards in Massachusetts and as CEO of the Girl Scouts of Eastern Massachusetts. In addition to her university leadership, Caitríona is the founder of nuxcrew, her own consulting and programmatic business dedicated to advancing wellness, leadership, and organizational effectiveness.

Her expertise is complemented by a diverse portfolio of current and past certifications, including Lifeguard Instructor Trainer, Water Safety Instructor, Group Exercise Instructor, Spinning Cycle Instructor, 500-Hour Registered Yoga Teacher, Worksite Wellness Specialist, and Campus of Difference Trainer.

Caitríona holds a bachelor's degree in international relations from Boston University, an MBA in Global Management, and a master's degree in Higher Education from Boston College. She is currently pursuing her EdD in the Boston University Higher Education Leadership program. She also serves on the NIRSA Services Corporation Board and Sports Network Board, helping shape strategic initiatives for collegiate recreation nationwide.

A dedicated mentor, consultant, and lifelong learner, Caitríona is committed to creating environments where people and organizations can thrive. She was born in Cork, Ireland, and resides in Massachusetts with her two-year-old triplets.

Connect with Caitríona:

LinkedIn: https://www.linkedin.com/in/caitrionataylor/

Website: https://www.nuxcrew.com/

Email: caitriona.taylor@gmail.com

CHAPTER SIXTEEN

GOING DEEPER

GETTING PAST PLATITUDES AS AN IMPACTFUL MENTOR

CAPT Chuck Hollingsworth, U.S. Navy (Ret.)

Remember that mentor leadership is all about serving.

~ Tony Dungy

*A mentor is not someone who walks ahead of us
and tells us how they did it. A mentor is someone who
walks alongside us to guide us on what we can do.*

~ Simon Sinek

MY STORY

Warning: Moving a relatively short-term mentoring relationship to an impactful depth is harder than it sounds.

Effective mentoring is a partnership between two willing individuals. The quality of this partnership relies on their ability to move past bumper-sticker leadership tenets and well-worn stories.

Even as a seasoned mentor, I had this nagging feeling that I was failing in my newest mentoring relationship. I couldn't help but wonder, *what's going wrong?*

My mentee, Sara, and I agreed on my favorite barbeque restaurant for our third mentorship meeting. Mission BBQ was a local favorite in this historic military town, known for its four-walled décor that honors the military and first responders. The aromas of slow-cooked brisket and smoked pork filled the room. There were quiet booths for personal discussions, and the laid-back atmosphere, combined with free drink refills, created an unhurried vibe. And while this was an evening meeting, I knew that earlier that day, every local Mission BBQ in the country paused at noon local time to play the national anthem. I liked that.

What I *didn't* like was the lack of progress in my current mentoring relationship. We met a few times before, and we had two previous one-on-one sessions that lasted more than an hour each. We did all the normal things to establish a baseline relationship. We shared our family histories and professional journeys, and it was clear to me that Sara, as a mid-career professional in a highly technical field, was interested in becoming a better leader. But something was missing.

I arrived at the restaurant a little early to gather my thoughts.

I'm a people person, but in this case, we just haven't clicked.

What stories, principles, and leadership nuggets have I shared thus far?

Why am I struggling to identify a clear mentorship strategy to help Sara in her quest?

My thoughts were interrupted by a cheery, "Hello," from Sara as she strode into the restaurant, right on time. I signaled for her to order her food and join me, then watched as she proceeded to the counter at the back of the restaurant.

Sara was in her early thirties, with shoulder-length brown hair and piercing blue eyes. She moved with the poise and confidence of a collegiate athlete. By all measures, she was a talented and successful young professional. Sara clearly held her own in a historically male-dominated engineering field, and she was approaching that critical career milestone where her leadership determined future success more than her technical competence. While technical acumen served her well thus far, the sometimes-elusive soft skills would determine the trajectory of her next decade in the workforce. Fortunately, she seemed to be acutely aware of this important transition on her horizon.

As she approached, I placed a mental wager.

I'll bet she has a salad instead of barbeque.

As she sat down, I smiled. She had a large dinner salad with a good portion of smoked turkey added to the top and a side of ranch dressing. We enjoyed a friendly conversation as we ate, catching up on current events and providing personal updates. We chatted briefly with a friendly table hostess and noticed the family-oriented crowd of patrons was beginning to thin as we moved past the normal dinner hour.

We cleared the table and retrieved our notebooks that contained the structured material we were supposed to cover during the session. But before we launched into a discussion on the material, I decided to take a different approach.

"Sara, is it okay with you if we just talk a bit before jumping into the material?"

"Absolutely," she replied. "What's on your mind?"

"I know we've covered several chapters of content already, but it dawned on me that I'd like to take a step back and talk about the bigger picture for a few minutes."

Sara carefully wiped the condensation off her drink, took a sip, then said, "Sure, I'm always happy to discuss anything you'd like."

With that, I asked in a very conversational tone, "Why did you join this leadership program? What's your core motivation?"

"Well," she answered, "I guess to be a better leader."

"That's great," I said. "Now, can you articulate for me *why* you want to be a better leader?"

She pondered that for a moment, "I think I can be more influential and effective, I guess."

"Okay, that makes sense." *Now is the time to dig deeper. I hope she doesn't get frustrated.* "Let me ask again: *Why* do you want to be more influential? What's the value of becoming a more influential leader?"

With that, Sara paused and visibly considered the question. After a brief reflection, she answered, "I guess it's because I want to be seen as a better leader, and therefore it will be better for my career progression."

Now we're getting to core motivations, so let's press a little deeper.

"I appreciate your candor, Sara, I really do. I have no doubt that applying the lessons from this program will help your career progression. But let me ask you: Have you considered the personal impact you'll have on those you're leading?"

Sara considered the question thoughtfully. "You know, to be honest, I don't think I have. I've looked at this through the lens of my own career opportunities, but I haven't really considered the personal impact on others."

Now we're getting somewhere, I told myself. *We want to encourage leaders to a life of selfless service, and to do that, we've got to help our leaders shift from a self-centered focus to an others-focus.*

She looked into her drink, clearly deep in thought. My impulse was to speak—I had so much to say. But my gut told me perhaps silence and contemplation were the best course of action in this moment.

Sara shook her head, as if clearing away a fog. She looked at me with a flash of recognition in her eyes. "Wow, I'm rethinking so many things right now. I feel a little foolish saying this, but I've viewed everything about my leader development through the lens of my own career and how I'm perceived. I haven't really considered those I'm charged to lead."

"That's okay," I encouraged. "It's human nature to view the world through one's personal lens. But the insight you've just expressed is a game-changer. If it's okay with you, let's continue the discussion with a conscious effort to consider the impact on those we're leading."

"Let's do it," Sara exclaimed, renewed purpose evident in her tone of voice and body language.

AN OBSERVATION

Moments of insight like the one depicted above are rare; the norm is typically much more subtle. However, the insight for me as a mentor was that it would've been easy to continue covering content, complete with my pithy stories and leadership catchphrases, and never go deep enough to get to my mentee's core motivations.

Sara wasn't the only one with a significant insight during this meeting. As I reflected on the evening, I faced my own motivations and approach as a mentor. Because the forces of human nature are always at work, it's worth taking a few minutes to unpack some considerations and strategies to ensure our mentoring efforts are on target.

THE STRATEGY

Let's remember: Leading isn't for wimps. It never has been, and it never will be.

Sometimes, leaders seeking personal and professional development can become absorbed with their *own* journey, and it's easy to forget about the profound impact leaders have on those they have the privilege of leading.

As mentors, we have a responsibility to remind those we're coaching that there's an ethical element to leadership. In the swirl of daily operations, leaders can forget they're truly impacting lives. They can forget they're a major influence on an employee's quality of life. Leaders can forget they're helping people realize their potential—or not. As mentors, *we* have a responsibility to guide leaders to a higher quality of leadership.

I passionately believe you wouldn't be a leadership mentor if you didn't care. So, as we remind ourselves of the weighty responsibility of leadership, let's challenge ourselves to the equally important responsibility that we assume as mentors. In light of this responsibility, let's explore some strategies that will help mentors in their effort to make the world a better place.

THE SEVEN C'S: A MENTOR'S COMPASS

Here are some strategies to empower you as a leadership mentor. As a sailor who has seen the world, I offer these strategies not as "seven seas," but as Seven C's.

1. Connection first.

- Establishing a connection with the mentee is an obvious, but important, first step to accomplish the rest of these strategies. Invest the time.

2. Core beliefs.

- Take time to contemplate and be able to articulate your core beliefs. Then, understand your mentee's core beliefs. This is foundational.

3. Critical assessment.

- A critical assessment of mentee motivation is paramount. Are they in it for themselves, or do they recognize the ethical nature of leadership?

4. Caution on dumping.

- Good mentors doubtless have countless stories, conference nuggets, and clickbait platitudes. But the mentee can experience your "tool bag" as more of a "dump truck." It's not intentional, but it's real.

5. Check ego.

- Checking your ego "at the door" is vital as a mentor. It's not about you and your incredible experience. Listen first, then offer only the most relevant information that promises to make an impact.

6. Coaching mindset.

- Mentors aren't there to replace the leader or even provide a model for the leader. We're there to coach. Listen, then coach. Rather than "telling," coach the mentee to reflect on insights. Insights drive change.

7. Counter entropy.

- Everything in the universe trends toward deterioration, including our own well-intentioned efforts to mentor. Am I investing in my mentee the way I once did? Am I taking shortcuts? Assuming, not listening? Guard yourself.

FINAL THOUGHTS

If you're reading this chapter, you're a special person.

You've experienced the burden and privilege of leadership, and you've gone one step further and made a commitment to help others on their leadership journey. As we established above, this isn't a commitment to take lightly. Whether you're a compensated mentor or a nonprofit volunteer, the privilege of helping someone achieve their human potential is a difficult concept on which to place a traditional valuation. By investing in one leader, you have the opportunity to impact the lives of many. The sobering reality is that the opposite is also true. Our failure to mentor to the best of our ability can result in a missed opportunity to help a leader realize their maximum potential.

Let's go back to that barbeque restaurant. Instead of reaching into my mentoring tool bag and grabbing the perfectly balanced tool for a specific moment in time, there's a tendency to simply back up the two-ton dump truck and pull that lever that raises the truck bed, allowing thousands of pounds of wisdom and experience to slide out onto the mentee in a torrent of "help" that's simply too much to absorb. It's too much to assimilate in a proper context. It's simply too much.

So why do we do it? In a strange paradox, it takes less thought and energy to pull the lever on a dump truck than it does to listen intently and determine what precise counsel is most appropriate for the moment. Let's be blunt: It's the easy way out. It's lazy.

And since we're getting deep and self-reflective, let's acknowledge another base element of human nature that can impact the quality of our mentoring: pride. A desire to show you just how much "stuff" I have in my dump truck reveals my potential for hubris. But if we flip the relationship, and make the development of the mentee the focus, then we're perfectly comfortable reaching into our tool bag and grabbing the small, slot screwdriver for just the right moment and application. In fact, it's quite possible this mentee may never know what a rich arsenal of tools I have to offer—and that's okay. As a thoughtful mentor, it's not about you or me. It's about the leader we're enabling.

With this final context in mind, I invite you to re-read the Seven C's above.

Pause a moment to consider these principles with serious self-reflection. Again, I presume you have both the desire and experience to make an incredible difference in another leader's life. And when you help another leader attain their potential, you're making the world a better place.

Thank you for that.

CAPT Chuck Hollingsworth, U.S. Navy (Ret.), is passionate about equipping others to lead. While Chuck spent most of his Navy career flying operational missions all over the globe, his non-flying assignments included significant training and mentoring positions. Chuck was hand-picked as the commanding officer of the Navy's Center for Personal and Professional Development, responsible for the leader development of more than 300,000 enlisted and commissioned officer sailors. He has been selected as a visionary leader by The Public Manager magazine and established a new operational fitness training resource for the U.S. Navy.

Chuck is published on ethical leadership and has been a presenter of best training practices at the American Society for Training and Development BEST Awards. He was a founding Board member of the Severn Leadership Group, a nonprofit leadership mentoring program for mid-career professionals. Additionally, Chuck continues to mentor countless veterans in their post-military transitions. In his current role, Chuck leads a professional development team for one of the largest defense contractors in the world.

While he often works in the Washington, D.C., area, Chuck lives in the hill country of his home state, Texas. He's active in church and veteran activities and remains dedicated to outdoor recreational sports and fitness. His most recent passion involves establishing a legacy of leadership, which he accomplishes by playing on the floor with his young grandchildren.

Connect with Chuck:

Facebook: https://www.facebook.com/ChuckHollingsworth/

Instagram: https://www.instagram.com/hollingsworthchuck/

LinkedIn: https://www.linkedin.com/in/chuckhollingsworth/

Email: chuck.t.hollingsworth@gmail.com

CHAPTER SEVENTEEN

THE A.R.T. OF LEADERSHIP

ACCOUNTABILITY, RESPONSIBILITY, AND TRANSPARENCY

Mark C. Germano, MBA, MS Ed. Psych.

The plot: My organization is the epicenter of a national scandal, and I'm embroiled in it by association. The characters: a local Fortune 100 CEO and me. The setting: his office. Because we live in a community of 250,000 people, I know him, where he lives, and his family. Conversely, he knows me, where I live, and my family. I work for the local United Way, and his corporation and their employees represent a little over 50% of all the charitable giving our organization receives on an annual basis.

MY STORY

"Well, how much money did you steal?" asked the CEO.

My initial reaction was stunned anger. One of my core principles throughout my life is honesty. And, when dealing with charitable gifts, I wanted to be extra careful with how our organization uses and deploys those gifts. Additionally, I felt personally insulted. *I knew—or thought I knew—this man.*

"I understand why you'd ask that question," I replied, "but I also know you and your family. You know me and my family. You know how much I get paid and what my benefit package looks like. What I can tell you is not one cent has been stolen or misappropriated in our local office. I invite anyone from your accounting department to come over and look at our books, expense reports, or any other financial documents they care to see." *I was seething inside. I wanted to show and prove to him and the WHOLE world, "I DID NOT STEAL! IT WASN'T ME!"*

This chapter is set in a nonprofit organization completely dependent on charitable giving. Charitable giving fuels over 1,500,000 nonprofit organizations in the United States. As Americans, we're incredibly generous people. According to *GivingUSA.org* we give over $550 billion annually.

I worked from one of the country's largest—and, at the time of this story in 1992, one of the most widely known and respected—charitable organizations: United Way. Over the decades, United Way evolved into a very efficient group of fundraising organizations with no or very small groups of paid staff members. Funds collected annually were then distributed to local nonprofit or faith-based service providers to address every human condition or issue. The recipients of those funds were called partner organizations. Over the decades, the United Ways across the country continued to be governed by local volunteers, but the need to hire paid staff became evident, and those paid staff needed to be professional, competent, and able to lead change in the delivery of human services in local communities across the country. A national association called United Way of America became the central hub for volunteer and paid staff training, and national initiatives to combat societal issues like alcoholism, domestic violence, positive youth development, aging with dignity, and many more.

In 1992, this network of local United Ways was raising and distributing over $2.2 billion. And the leader of the national association was a very dynamic, charismatic man who had been a part of the growth and professionalism of local United Ways for more than 30 years. While this leader, William Aramony, was lauded for the many innovations he brought to the nonprofit industry, over time, he became more arrogant, and believed sincerely that if United Way was going to attract volunteers from the C-suite levels of corporate America, then he needed to act, behave and be compensated like those people.

Why is it important for you to understand the structure? Because every organization has a structure. Every organization must function as a team. Team leadership is essential to success. And, if you examine any successful team in any walk of life, you know they face challenges, and sometimes a crisis. Good teams and good team leaders can get the team, not just themselves, through the challenge and ultimately to a higher level of performance.

AT THE EPICENTER OF A NATIONAL SCANDAL

In this case, the United Way of America (UWA) found itself in the center of a scandal that ultimately resulted in the national CEO, CFO, and bookkeeper going to federal prison and paying back millions of dollars in restitution. And it didn't happen quietly. It made national and local news.

On Sunday, February 16, 1992, Jack Anderson, noted and respected columnist for the *Washington Post*, wrote an editorial accusing UWA's CEO of misusing donor dollars and poked an accusatory finger at its board of directors for failing to fulfill their fiduciary oversight responsibilities. Immediately, local newspapers, radio, and television stations also ran the same story with numerous requests for local interviews. At this time, fax machines were the most efficient and rapid means of information distribution. On Monday, February 17, every local United Way office in the country received a long fax from the national CEO categorically denying any of Jack Anderson's charges.

When I read the Jack Anderson column, and then read the fax denying all the charges, my first thought was, "Damn, Aramony did it!" And the next thought I had was, "I hope it goes away soon." I was right and wrong.

Investigative journalists at the *Wall Street Journal, New York Times, Washington Post, Miami Herald, Baltimore Sun,* NBC, ABC, and CBS demanded to see all UWA's financial records and expense reports, especially the national CEO's expenses, salary, employee benefits, etc. Unfortunately, the national CEO attempted to stonewall the journalists' efforts, which only amplified their determination. At the same time, local, regional, and national media outlets approached their local United Way offices asking for the same information.

Since United Way developed a very efficient fundraising and fund distribution model based on local needs, corporate and community leaders served on the local board of directors as fundraising and fund distribution chair(s). It was typical to have the community's top ten to 20 corporate and community leaders in visible, prominent roles within each local United Way. For example, I was 33 years old at this time, and I had personally known and worked with Fortune 100 CEOs, national celebrities, NFL players, and numerous national and local media. My children hated going grocery shopping with me because, invariably, I would be stopped at least three times in the store by community members asking about their favorite nonprofit. Or asking me to get involved with their personal community initiative. Frankly, at this stage of my career, it was flattering and a real boost to my ego. At times, I thought to myself, *"This is amazing. I'm just a small-town kid being asked my opinion by people that I read about in the newspaper. Amazing!"*

For an organization whose roots were built over 100 years on local control and local autonomy, the directives from UWA to not disclose financial information were roundly rejected. Local United Ways demanded the same type of information from UWA. Initially, UWA refused to release financial information to local organizations. The local United Ways responded by suspending or completely stopping dues payments to UWA. On February 27, UWA's CEO and two other individuals involved in the scandal, including the past and current CFO, resigned. UWA's board of directors appointed an interim CEO.

Pressure continued to build from local United Ways toward UWA for a full accounting and disclosure of all relevant financial information. Ultimately, UWA's board convened a meeting of 50 executive directors representing the 1,700 local United Ways to lay out a collective course of action.

The 50 local executive directors, of which I was one, voted unanimously to pursue a trial.

Because United Way was so well known and respected, there were intense and constant calls for answers. Additionally, there was an ever-growing number of questions from local media, volunteers, partner agencies, and donors about how money was being used locally. For example, our local United Way was featured in the local paper 57 times in one year, with six of those stories being front-page, above-the-fold articles. Numerous radio and television interviews were requested and given. Initially, the September campaign giving was down nearly 20%. The fundraising campaign only lasted seven weeks, and I was scared we would not be anywhere near our fundraising goal. If those initial fundraising results continued at that rate, partner agencies' grants would have to be cut or eliminated, local United Way staff would have to be let go, or a combination of both. Regardless of the local board's decisions, people's lives would be affected.

WHAT WOULD YOU DO?

If you've read this far, what would you do? You have a responsibility to lead people—an organization—and to be of service, but everybody doubts you. People are angry. On a cognitive level, you can understand that. But we're made up of thoughts and feelings. And it's those feelings that wake you up at two o'clock in the morning, trying to figure out an answer, but the hamster wheel just keeps spinning.

This was the first time I had to deal with a "scandal" and bear the brunt of the accusations, recriminations, and suspicions of people I thought I knew and trusted. It was also the first time I realized I was accountable and responsible for the actions and statements of anyone at the local, regional, or national level who identified themselves as a United Way volunteer, staff, or donor. Frankly, I was overwhelmed. I kept thinking to myself, *I didn't do it. It was Bill Aramony. We've run a very clean operation. Damn it, stop staring at me like I am a thief.* But that was my initial reaction. Eating "humble pie" is not a bad thing. I soon learned that a truly great team leader is also a humble person. And, humility does not mean meekness, but instead means a willingness to learn. To be open to new ideas, new approaches. To truly move way outside one's comfort zone.

Another important lesson I learned during that time was that initial negative reactions far outweigh positive or supportive statements.

Coincidentally, during this crisis, I attended a management seminar, and one of the speakers was the vice president of customer delight at Chili's. Their research showed that every diner who had a negative experience influenced, on average, 223 people. And every diner who had a positive experience influenced, on average, 24 people. So, negative comments and thoughts will generate approximately ten times more than positive ones. That really stuck in my head and helped me, and my team, understand what people in our community might be thinking and saying. And to also continue to put out all the facts as we knew them. To hammer home the facts and not just react, or worse, overreact to a rumor.

LEADERSHIP IMPLICATIONS

Due to my training as a research psychologist, I understand the concept of the "fight or flight" center of our brains. It's an ancient mechanism we used to survive as homo sapiens. Today, it manifests through a great deal of negative news and social media posts. If you look at your news sources and social media, and count the number of posts you think are negative versus those that are positive, I believe you'll find that ratio is present.

So, what does this have to do with leadership? What you must be prepared for—and prepare your team for—is the reality that you, your team, your work product, or someone associated with your organization will generate negative news. It may be internal. It may be external. It may generate a small ripple in you or your team's performance. Or, it may have such a large impact that it brings down your organization.

No one ever thinks that's possible. But our history is replete with organizations that have fallen due to hubris, mismanagement, or an unwillingness to be accountable, responsible, and transparent.

If you doubt me, look up companies like Enron, Arthur Anderson, Madoff Investments, or E.F. Hutton. I wager none of those companies' leaders ever imagined a day when they'd go out of business—or, even worse, be prosecuted for criminal activities.

Poor performance or leadership doesn't just happen overnight. When you look back at what happened in these organizations, you often see that entry and mid-level employees started to warn upper management about issues long before they became major problems.

No one is perfect, and there will be days or situations where you make mistakes. That's okay. Admit those mistakes and seek ways not to repeat them moving forward. That means you have to be willing to accept feedback. And that's not always an easy thing to do. None of us wants to admit we have weaknesses or faults. All of us like to focus on our positive attributes. It's our human nature. But those people who are willing to be responsible, transparent, and held accountable for their actions and words will excel.

THE STRATEGY

THE A.R.T. OF LEADERSHIP

Accountability: Willingness to answer for your, your team's, and your organization's actions.

Responsibility: Willingness to deal with something, or to have control over yourself, your team, and your organization.

Transparency: Openness to public scrutiny.

THINGS CAN GET MESSY, BUT THE TRUTH ALWAYS COMES OUT

I was a nonprofit executive director in a mid-sized, Midwest community. And yet, I received national attention and very pointed questions directed at me and others in our organization. When you're the leader, people look to you for answers.

My very strong recommendation: Tell the truth as best you know it at that time. If you don't know the answer, then tell people when you'll get it. For example, when I got questions and I didn't have the facts, I said I would get back to them in 24 hours. Even if I had to tell them I needed more time, I always followed up. This is what accountability, responsibility, and transparency mean. You can't pawn things off and just be around for the good stuff.

You may think you're the only one going through something difficult in your work life. You're not. In numerous cases, a manager, director, vice president, or CEO of a company finds themselves in a difficult situation. UWA's crisis could have been an internal issue, but in this case, it became a national scandal with a very public trial. The perpetrators were found guilty, and they served their entire sentences. They got no time off for good behavior. Additionally, they had to pay back double what they took.

A leadership mentor that I respect has a saying, "Only mold and deceit grow in the dark." As a current or future leader, you must be as accountable, responsible, and transparent as necessary. When leading your team(s), share the facts as best you know them at that time. Yes, as you get better data, things may change. You owe it to yourself and to those you work with to be as clear and candid as possible.

Leadership is messy. Problems and issues develop with people, processes, and programs or products. That is a fact of life and leadership. So, don't be surprised if you get a call at night or on the weekend about something that makes your stomach clench.

You can work your way through it as long as you don't try to do it all by yourself. Use your resources, mentors, data, family, friends, and your faith to help you and your team through the challenge. Do not try to be the "smartest person in the room." Use authentic listening to help you understand people's concerns, and work with your team to chart a path forward. Build milestones into that path forward and be sure to CELEBRATE SUCCESS ALONG THE WAY. All too often, we do not celebrate our successes. But take the time to celebrate your team's successes. It will help you and them when you encounter the next obstacle.

The individuals who usually fail are those who try to solve things all by themselves or think "…they are the smartest person in the room." Why? Because, eventually, the team stops working and supporting them. No one wants to work for someone who is only centered on themselves. They may do it for a while, but ultimately, people leave. People want to be successful. They want to be part of a successful team. If only the leaders are successful, the organization will ultimately implode. Dictators always fall.

TOOLS FOR A.R.T.FUL LEADERS

During the UWA crisis, I dealt with people much more powerful, richer, and with significantly higher profiles than me. It didn't make them better than me, but at times, I felt intimidated. You may find yourself in that same situation. You must be true to yourself. You have to learn what your strengths are and admit your weaknesses. I'm good at data analysis, but I'm not very good at understanding people's emotional reactions to situations. I like to look at the data and search for the logic in it. Again, we're human and logical, but we're also emotional. And our emotions can overwhelm us or others.

The tool I've found to be the most helpful for me is something called the Emotional Quotient Inventory. It's a wonderful tool that helps me understand my emotions, how others react to me, and how I react to various situations. I discovered it at age 64 and have been using it ever since. The inventory is a good tool; what makes it great is having a trained facilitator to help you understand the results and help with strategies and tactics to improve your insights, yourself, and your team.

Seek out assistance, and you will be amazed at how people will help you when you least expect it. If you have a mentor, talk with them regularly, not just during the crisis. If you don't have a mentor, find one.

START ON YOUR A.R.T. PROJECT NOW

Our media, literature, and social media are filled with examples of people who have used the A.R.T. of leadership. Yes, they've failed. Yes, they've suffered public and private defeats, but they continued to pursue the best in themselves and others. A few exemplars of the A.R.T. of leadership are Abraham Lincoln, Dr. Martin Luther King, Jr., Billie Jean King, and Ann Dunwoody, the Army's first four-star general.

I had the honor of sitting beside retired General Dunwoody on a two-hour plane ride. I had no idea who she was or her background. Being a social guy, I struck up a conversation with her. She was so humble and forthright, it truly was a conversation I'll never forget. I asked her what one thing she learned about leadership. She said, "Never walk by a mistake.

When you do, you immediately lose credibility with those you serve with, and you become prone to walking by them in the future."

So, how can you get started? I encourage you to get a binder or notebook and write one thing you did today that exemplified accountability, responsibility, or transparency. It might be something as simple as submitting your expense report on time, or as important as having a difficult conversation with an underperforming employee. But make a note of it each day. At the end of each week, look at what you accomplished. Over time, you will become an A.R.T.ist in leadership.

Start now.

Mark Germano is an experienced executive with nearly 50 years of experience leading complex organizations at the national, state, and local levels. He has personally raised more than $700 million in philanthropic donations during his career and conducted 35,000 successful philanthropic gift solicitations. Mark has closed over 100 seven- and eight-figure philanthropic gifts, including an extensive number of transformational gifts for all types of nonprofit organizations and communities of faith. He works with clients from all 50 U.S. states and 69 countries. He has trained over 6,000 individuals on all aspects of nonprofit marketing, fundraising, and generating sustainable, renewable revenue.

Throughout his career, Mark has worked with over 250 nonprofit and education consulting clients. His work includes leading organizations through strategic planning, all forms of fundraising, creating regional collaborations and mergers, marketing, program outcome evaluation initiatives, and innovating grant-making processes. He has extensive nonprofit board, volunteer, electronic, and print media training, and is a public speaking trainer and crisis communication spokesperson.

Mark received his master's degree in business administration-marketing from Roosevelt University, Chicago, a master's degree in educational psychology from the University of Wisconsin–Madison, and a bachelor's degree in psychology from Kent State University. His certifications include Certified Mentor by the Severn Leadership Group and Certified EQi administrator and facilitator.

Mark's professional and community affiliations include founder and president of Creating Solutions, a consulting firm for nonprofits, non-governmental organizations, and communities of faith; United States Naval Academy Blue and Gold Officer (BGO) since 2008; member of the Wisconsin Service Academies Selection Review Board since 2015; adjunct instructor, University of Notre Dame, Mendoza School of Business; speaker at venture capital/angel funding forums in Chicago, Philadelphia, New York, Silicon Valley, Minneapolis/St. Paul, Dallas, Atlanta, Raleigh-Durham, Washington, D.C., and a past board member, Severn Leadership Group.

Connect with Mark:

Website: https://www.facebook.com/solutions4nonprofits

LinkedIn: https://www.linkedin.com/in/mcgermano/

Email: mark@creatingsolutions.info

CHAPTER EIGHTEEN

FORGED FOR THIS

RISING FROM THE CRUCIBLE

Dr. Mike Jefferson

If God be for us, who can be against us?

~ Romans 8:31

I can do all things, through Christ who strengthens me.

~ Philippians 4:13

PRELUDE: A JOURNEY OF RESILIENCE, MENTORSHIP, AND UNWAVERING FAITH

In the crucible of life, where the fires of adversity burn hottest, true strength is not merely found; it is forged. This is a story of such a forging, a testament to the human spirit's capacity not just to endure, but to transform profound devastation into a foundation for unparalleled growth. It's a journey through the depths of personal and professional collapse, illuminated by the unwavering light of faith and the guiding hand of mentorship.

MY STORY

THE UNIMAGINABLE STORM

October 2011. The very mention of that month still sends a chill down my spine. It was then that a brutal storm descended upon my life, unleashing a series of personal and professional tragedies I could never have imagined. My world, meticulously built on discipline and unwavering commitment, began to unravel with a terrifying swiftness.

THE ASCENT: A LIFE OF PURPOSE AND PROMISE

For as long as I can remember, my life has been a testament to disciplined ambition. From the moment I stepped onto the hallowed grounds of the U.S. Naval Academy, I was driven by a singular purpose: to serve with excellence and rise through the ranks. My career in the U.S. Navy Supply Corps was a steady ascent, marked by hard work, consistent excellence, and a relentless pursuit of innovation.

My fitness reports, the Navy's rigorous evaluations, were consistently unparalleled, painting a picture of an officer destined for the highest echelons. I was postured for Captain, the pinnacle of a naval career, a testament to decades of dedication. *I felt invincible, my path clear and undeniable.*

My days were a symphony of strategic planning, logistical execution, and leadership development. I thrived on challenges, seeing every obstacle as an opportunity to refine processes and inspire my teams. As a change agent, I wasn't content with the status quo; I sought to optimize, to innovate, to push the boundaries of what was possible within the Navy's bureaucratic complexities. I believed true leadership meant not just maintaining the ship, but actively charting a more efficient, more impactful course.

This drive, while yielding exceptional results and glowing fitness reports, also, unbeknownst to me, sowed seeds of friction. My unconventional approach, while effective, sometimes ruffled feathers among those who preferred tradition over transformation. This dynamic, where an individual's drive for progress clashes with an established, hierarchical system, often creates a unique form of professional adversity.

The very qualities that propelled me forward—my inclination to challenge and improve—became a source of resistance from senior leaders. A change agent's journey within such a structure often becomes a crucible in itself, tempering one's resolve not just against external challenges, but against the friction generated by your authentic self.

THE UNRAVELING: A CASCADE OF CRISES

Then, the world as I knew it began to unravel—not with a single blow, but with a relentless, compounding series of seismic shifts. It was as if the universe decided to test the very limits of my resolve, all at once. The simultaneous arrival of multiple, severe challenges can create an impact exponentially greater than the sum of individual adversities. When foundational life pillars—career identity, family stability, parental support— begin to collapse simultaneously, psychological and emotional resources can be completely depleted, leading to a profound state of overwhelm.

First, the professional storm clouds gathered. My nature as a change agent, once a source of pride and success, became a target. I felt the subtle, then overt, chill from senior officers, their ridicule and persecution a constant, draining undercurrent. The qualities that propelled me forward now seemed to hold me back. I pushed for innovation, for efficiency, for a better way, but the resistance was fierce, and it felt deeply personal. This professional siege was a constant drain, chipping away at my confidence and sense of purpose. *Was all my hard work for nothing? The question echoed in my mind, a relentless drumbeat of doubt.*

Concurrently with this professional siege, my world imploded. The call came, piercing my heart and soul, that my beloved mother, Nina, had passed away unexpectedly. The grief was a physical weight, crushing, leaving me breathless and lost. Before I could even begin to process this profound loss, another devastating blow struck: My then-spouse was diagnosed with bipolar disorder. The diagnosis itself was a shock, but the immediate aftermath was a whirlwind of manic energy, culminating in a demand for divorce. The emotional landscape of my home, once a sanctuary, became a battlefield of unpredictable highs and lows, ending in an agonizing separation. The convergence of these deeply personal tragedies and professional challenges created relentless pressure, pushing me to my absolute limits.

THE ABYSS: WHEN HOPE FADES

As if these personal and professional earthquakes weren't enough, the tremors continued in my career. The path to Captain, which I meticulously paved with years of unparalleled dedication, suddenly seemed blocked. I was passed over for command, the surest way to secure that next promotion.

A cold dread settled in my stomach. *Is this the end of the road I so diligently built?* Then, the ultimate professional rejection: I was passed over for Captain during my first look for promotion.

Devastated. The word barely captures the crippling sense of failure, loss, and exhaustion that consumed me. My career, my family, my very sense of self—everything I had worked for, everything I held dear, seemed to crumble all at once. *I questioned everything. Is my hard work meaningless? Was my belief in myself misplaced?*

This period was a true *abyss*, a time when the ground beneath me felt like quicksand. The future, once a clear path, became a dense fog, obscuring even the outline of what I once envisioned. The cumulative weight of these coinciding adversities created a crisis that was not merely a setback, but a seismic shift that scrambled my internal compass and unveiled doubts I never knew I had.

THE TURNING POINT: LEANING INTO LIGHT

In that abyss of despair, when the darkness felt absolute, a flicker of light emerged. It wasn't a sudden, blinding revelation, but a quiet, persistent whisper of resolve. I knew I couldn't stay in that darkness. I had to find a way back, a way through.

I leaned on the pillars of strength I had always cherished, though perhaps not fully appreciated until then: my mentor, my family, my confidante. Their encouragement and empowerment were the lifelines that pulled me from the deepest waters. They didn't offer easy answers, but they offered unwavering belief. And then, the spiritual awakening. In my lowest moment, I turned to the ultimate source of strength. I prayed to God, pouring out every ounce of my pain and despair. A profound sense of peace, a quiet conviction, settled over me. I made up my mind: "*If God be for me, who can be against me?*" This wasn't just a thought; it was a re-anchoring, a spiritual recalibration.

When all external support—career, family, social structures—proves insufficient or crumbles entirely, an internal, spiritual foundation becomes not just a comfort, but the ultimate source of stability and empowerment. This re-orientation of perspective, shifting the locus of control from chaotic external circumstances to an unwavering internal alignment with a higher power, allowed me to find the resilience needed to move forward.

I put on my optimistic hat, not as a denial of pain, but as a conscious choice to pursue my next victory and the drive to overcome with all that was in me, to be better and achieve my next best thing. This holistic approach, combining external support with internal spiritual and psychological work, became a potent "elixir" for overcoming such profound adversity.

The crucible of personal battles, though agonizing, became the forge that tempered my spirit. Lessons learned in that intense heat were not just for me; they're universal principles for anyone facing their moments of profound uncertainty. My journey from devastation to defiant optimism crystallized into a powerful framework, an "*elixir of overcoming*" that can be applied to any challenge. It's a strategy for not just surviving, but thriving, when the world shifts beneath your feet.

THE STRATEGY

The path to rising from adverse uncertainty to becoming truly *"forged for this"* isn't a passive journey. It demands active engagement, a willingness to step into the heat, and the wisdom to seek guidance.

Drawing from personal experience and the profound insights articulated in several of my studies over the years, such as the Bible and various leadership and organizational transformation books, this strategy provides a practical framework for transforming personal crucibles into catalysts for growth. It's an exercise in self-mastery and strategic engagement with the forces that shape individuals.

EMBRACING THE FORGE: REDEFINING ADVERSITY

The first step to overcome adversity is to shift perspective. Adversity isn't merely a setback; it's a seismic shift that scrambles our internal compass and unveils doubts we never knew we had. Instead of shrinking, understand this is the very process that shapes, purifies, and transforms us into something infinitely stronger and more purposeful.

The metaphor of a blacksmith at the forge illustrates this process: A raw piece of iron, subjected to intense fire and the resounding blows of a hammer, doesn't break. Instead, it's shaped, purified, and transformed into something infinitely stronger and more purposeful. This understanding invites us to step into the forge, not as victims, but as the raw material for their next, most powerful iteration.

- Exercise: The Adversity Reframe

  - Grab a notebook and pen. Write down the adverse uncertainty currently faced or recently experienced.

  - Next, for each challenge, reframe it. Instead of "This is destroying me," ask: *How is this shaping me? What hidden strengths is this revealing? What new direction might this force me to take?*

  - This simple act of questioning, of seeking the "why" and "how" of transformation, begins to rewire the brain from problem-focused paralysis to solution-oriented action, much like the "affirmations" discussed in the context of shifting mindsets from negative statements to empowering questions.

THE MASTER FORGER'S TOUCH: CULTIVATING TRANSFORMATIVE MENTORSHIP

In moments of profound uncertainty, the question becomes: "But who holds the hammer? Who guides the process?" Often, it's a mentor. A mentor isn't just a coach; they're a "master forger" who sees the potential in an individual's struggle and shows them how to wield the hammer themselves.

The journey through the depths of despair is often only possible because one leans on a mentor, family, and confidants. These relationships provide an external perspective and unwavering belief when one's internal compass is spinning wildly.

A critical function of mentorship in times of severe adversity is its role in helping the individual reconstruct their understanding of painful experiences. Adversity frequently shatters an individual's self-narrative, leading to feelings of brokenness or failure. A mentor acts as a co-author, guiding the individual to weave these fragmented, traumatic threads into a coherent, empowering story of growth, learning, and triumph. This re-narration is fundamental for psychological healing, reclaiming agency, and building a foundation for future success, transforming the past from a burden into a source of strength.

- **Exercise: Identify Your Forging Team.** Reflect on the different types of support you may need, such as:

  ○ **The Seasoned Veteran:** Someone who has navigated similar crises and emerged stronger. Their practical advice and lived experience are invaluable.

  ○ **The Industry Innovator:** If a field is shifting, someone at the forefront of change can offer crucial insights into new directions and necessary skills.

  ○ **The Emotional Anchor:** Sometimes, you simply need someone who listens, validates feelings, and reminds you of your inherent strength. This might be a trusted friend, family member, or therapist.

List individuals who embody these roles or consider whom to seek out. Remember, mentorship doesn't always have to be a formal, long-term relationship. Sometimes, a single insightful conversation can be a forging moment.

Table: The Mentor's Forge: Guiding Your Transformation

Mentor's Role (The Hammer's Strike)	What It Addresses (The Raw Iron's Challenge)	Actionable Step (Your Shaping Response)	Impact (The Tempered Outcome)
Recalibrating Your Lens: Seeing Beyond the Smoke	Tunnel vision, fear, anxiety, inability to see possibilities beyond immediate threat	Seek outside perspectives, reframe narrative from "destroying me" to "shaping me." Identify hidden opportunities	Clarity, renewed hope, and identification of new pathways
Sharpening Your Inner Tools: Skills for the New Landscape	Skill gaps, outdated approaches, and rigidity in changing environments	Identify new skills needed, explore tangential fields, foster continuous learning, and agile response	Adaptability, enhanced capabilities, and readiness for future challenges
The Anchor of Belief: Accountability and Support	Self-doubt, procrastination, loss of momentum, feeling broken or inadequate	Set clear, achievable goals; engage in regular check-ins; allow mentors to mirror your strengths and remind you of past successes	Sustained momentum, unwavering confidence, and belief in self
Crafting Your Narrative: From Pain to Purpose	Fragmented self-narrative, trauma, and inability to integrate difficult experiences	Reflect on lessons learned; articulate your journey from adversity to resilience; transform traumatic experiences into a testament to strength	Psychological healing, profound self-awareness, and an empowering personal story

THE INNER CRUCIBLE: FORGING PERSONAL RESILIENCE

While external guidance is vital, the ultimate transformation happens within. The turning point often comes when an individual leans on their faith, making a conscious decision to shift their mindset and pursue their "*next victory*." This inner work is the quenching and tempering that solidifies resolve.

Resilience and overcoming adversity aren't a one-time achievement or a destination. Instead, they're an ongoing, iterative cycle of facing challenges (the "*heat*"), making conscious choices and taking action (the "*shaping*"), experiencing setbacks (the "*quenching*"), and learning from those setbacks to re-enter the process with greater strength. True mastery of overcoming lies in embracing this continuous cycle of transformation, viewing every future trial not as a failure, but as another opportunity for further tempering and refinement of the spirit.

FAITH AS YOUR FOUNDATION: SPIRITUAL ANCHORS AND AFFIRMATIONS

When everything else crumbles, an internal, spiritual anchor becomes paramount. A personal mantra, such as "*If God be for me, who can be against me,*" can become a bedrock.

Exercise: Your Personal Anchor

Identify a spiritual truth, core belief, or powerful affirmation that resonates deeply. This can be a scripture, a philosophical statement, or a personal creed. Write it down. Repeat it daily, especially when doubt or despair creeps in. Let it become the unwavering truth that cuts through the noise of uncertainty. This aligns with the use of biblical verses (John 16:33, Matthew 17:20, John 15:2) as powerful reminders of resilience and hope.

Mindset Mastery: Shifting from Despair to Drive

The shift from feeling so low to putting on an optimistic hat is a conscious act of mindset mastery. It's about retraining the brain, catching negative habits, and flipping the switch.

Exercise: The Optimistic Pivot

Whenever a negative thought or feeling of defeat arises, pause. Acknowledge the feeling without judgment. Then, consciously pivot. Ask: *What's the next best thing I can do right now? What small victory can I pursue? How can I reframe this challenge as an opportunity?* This proactive questioning, much like the affirmations mentioned, trains the brain to seek solutions and possibilities.

Action in Ambiguity: Decisive Steps Forward

In uncertainty, there's rarely a perfect answer. Even small, decisive steps forward, fueled by an optimistic outlook, create momentum.

Exercise: The Micro-Action Plan

Identify one area of life currently gripped by uncertainty. Break down any large, overwhelming problem into the smallest possible, actionable step that can be taken *today*. This isn't about solving everything; it's about initiating movement. For example, if overwhelmed by career uncertainty, a micro-action might be to research one potential new industry or update one section of your resume. Take that step, no matter how small.

A good plan, violently executed now,
is better than a perfect plan next week.

~ General George S. Patton

THE TEMPERED SPIRIT: LIVING *"FORGED FOR THIS"*

A painful journey can leave an individual with unshakeable resilience, a profound clarity of purpose, and a deeper sense of connection to those who walk alongside them. When the final sparks settle, the leader who emerges isn't simply a reassembled former self, but a being utterly transformed—a living testament to the power of perseverance and reflective evolution. This is the promise of becoming *"forged for this."*

- **Unshakeable Resilience.** Individuals don't simply resist the weight of life's challenges; they use every trial to propel themselves further. Like a resilient tree weathering mighty gales, each hardship integrates into the core, rendering them capable of not just surviving future storms but thriving because of them.

- **Enhanced Clarity of Purpose.** Amid the chaos, crises often strip life down to its bare essentials. Clarity discards the extraneous and reveals what truly matters. Professional setbacks, though devastating, can force a redefinition of success beyond titles and external validation, leading to a deeper purpose in mentoring and faith-based leadership.

- **Profound Self-Awareness.** Through the furnace of challenges, individuals gain intimate knowledge of their strengths and vulnerabilities. This self-awareness isn't manufactured overnight; it's earned through the raw process of facing and overcoming adversity.

- **Agility and Innovation**. In the cauldron of continual change, rigidity is a liability. A tempered leader embraces flexibility, reimagining and reinventing what already exists. A change agent's nature, once a source of friction, can become a refined tool for navigating new landscapes.

- **A Deeper Sense of Connection.** Finally, the journey reveals the undeniable power of human connection. In moments when the cold shadow of despair looms, a mentor's support and the camaraderie of those who share similar trials become a beacon of light. Reliance on mentors, family, and confidantes is not a weakness, but the ultimate strength.

"The only way to reach your highest potential is to have a mentor."

~ Dr. Mike Jefferson

The art of forging is eternal, a dynamic continuum where every trial, every surge of life's tumult, ultimately refines the spirit, ensuring the flame of resilience never fades but burns ever brighter. This narrative is but one example; every individual's journey awaits its next transformation.

Dr. Mike Jefferson is a transformative author whose journey blends the rigor of a 31-year U.S. Navy career with a passion for mentoring and faith-based leadership. A 1995 graduate of the U.S. Naval Academy with a B.S. in Economics, he also holds an M.B.A. in Financial Management, an M.S. in National Resource Strategy, and a Doctorate in Pastoral Leadership.

Throughout his naval tenure, Dr. Jefferson excelled in strategic and operational roles. As Supply Officer aboard USS Mount Vernon (LSD 39), his team earned the prestigious Blue "E" and Ney Awards. He later served as a maritime logistics officer for NATO Spanish Maritime Forces and deputy maritime operations officer at U.S. Central Command. He was the U.S. Pacific Fleet's operational logistics leader, followed by his final military role as senior supply officer at the U.S. Naval Academy. A fully Joint Qualified Officer and Acquisition Corps member, he's an expert in inventory planning, just-in-time purchasing, and strategic negotiations.

Committed to developing future leaders, Dr. Jefferson mentors through the Severn Leadership Group. Now, he extends his leadership and faith as the Men's Pastor and CFO at Transformation Christian Fellowship in Annapolis Junction, Maryland. A devoted family man—married to Ms. LaSonya Williams, father to three adult children, and grandfather to three—Dr. Jefferson's writing illuminates a path of resilience, insight, and continuous growth. His work inspires readers to transform challenges into stepping stones toward enduring excellence.

Connect with Mike:

Website: http://bit.ly/475gXCt

LinkedIn: https://www.linkedin.com/in/drmikej

Instagram: https://www.instagram.com/mikejeff72

CHAPTER NINETEEN

WINNING HEARTS AND MINDS

INSPIRING EXTRAORDINARY PERFORMANCE

Ray L. Steinmetz, SLG Mentor, Project Executive

Take care of your people and they will take care of you.

~ Old adage

To be an impactful leader and mentor, you need to win the hearts and minds of those you lead and mentor by developing *caring* relationships. You need to express it, and you need to demonstrate it, i.e., *walk the talk*. This chapter is about finding ways to make those connections and develop those relationships. I will start my story in an unlikely place: a giant shipyard in South Korea.

MY STORY

"Your expectations are unrealistic and way over the top on safety. You don't understand our operations."

But a worker just died!

I led a major project to design, build, and install a very large energy facility offshore Africa. The project's centerpiece involved constructing a 20,000-ton mass of steel, piping, and equipment with a footprint about the size of a football field and the height of a 20-story building. We awarded the construction contract to a shipyard in South Korea.

The shipyard was amazing, particularly to this structural engineer. I walked around the yard and marveled at the size, scale, and efficiency of the operation. *Wow! I had been on a lot of construction sites around the world, but nothing like this. What a masterful orchestration of a lot of huge moving parts!*

As far as I could see in every direction, towering cranes lifted blocks of sections of ships, huge forklifts buzzed around carrying all sorts of equipment, sparks flew from hundreds of workers grinding and welding pieces of steel together, and several 1000+-ft. ships in various stages of construction stood in assembly line fashion, outfitted with diesel engines the size of houses.

The yard was truly a world-class facility. At the time, it was one of three shipyards in South Korea that were churning out 60% of all the new ships in the world.

Having said all that, the shipyard was not world-class in safety culture. When I checked into my hotel just outside the yard's front gate, I heard chanting and someone yelling over a bullhorn. I looked out my window and saw a couple hundred workers carrying signs outside the gates. I asked the hotel manager, "What's going on?" "They're protesting the working conditions," he said. "A worker died on the job recently."

My company's and my team's expectations on our job were clear: *nobody gets hurt*, let alone dies. We knew we had a challenge in winning the hearts and minds of the shipyard's management. Before starting the job, we engaged at all levels of leadership, laying out our expectations for workforce safety and discussing how to achieve it, including multi-day workshops with their top management. Besides being the right thing to do, we demonstrated how *good safety is good business*.

We made some progress on winning their minds, but not so much their hearts. They seemed to be thinking, *these guys are just chasing safety statistics for their company's reputation*. We, in fact, heard them call us "a bunch of safety monks," which we were quite proud of, by the way.

We also spent a lot of time penetrating the shipyard's organization by conducting safety training and explicitly expressing care for the well-being of our workers. Again, we thought we were making some progress on their minds, but not so much on their hearts.

Good progress, but was it enough to get the job done without anyone getting hurt?

One of my on-site team members suggested, "How about we try to get the workers' families involved in changing the safety culture?" He proposed a friendly competition between the workers' children by inviting them to draw pictures of their parents working safely, e.g., wearing safety helmets and boots, tying off with their safety harnesses at heights, etc. The contest was a hit, generating lots of participation and energy. We published all the drawings along with photos of the children. Unquestionably, it helped us better connect and demonstrated caring for workers and their families.

But the real tipping point occurred when we posted the children's photos on a large banner, hung the banner over the entrance of the work site, and labeled it *Great Reasons to Work Safely.* Then, every day when the workers came walking onto the site, they looked up at the banner to see photos of their children or their coworkers' children and be reminded of the importance of working safely.

We truly connected! We finished the job with no fatalities, no lost time incidents, and just one medical treatment incident (a cut hand, no stitches) with hundreds of workers onsite for 16 months. And we delivered the project on time and within the budget, with excellent quality of workmanship—extraordinary results, particularly compared to the job going on right next to us in the yard. Another company built a very similar facility in scope and size to ours, and they suffered two fatalities, a dozen lost time incidents, and chose not to display their medical treatment incidents.

One day at the end of the job, I stood with the head of the shipyard (who had participated in our early safety workshops), comparing the safety board signs in front of the two sites. I asked him, "How can you explain the difference in results?"

"Oh," he said, "it is client-driven."

Somewhat disappointed in his response, I replied, "It shouldn't be. You could and should make this happen on all your job sites." I walked off with my best safety monk swagger.

With that demonstrated success, I extended the concept of posting photos of workers' children and spouses, labelled *Great Reasons to Work Safely*, to all our project sites worldwide. I still have a framed picture hanging in my home office today with photos of the children and spouses, including my own, from my last project site, as a great reminder for me to stay safe and healthy.

This story is also a great reminder that an idea can come from anyone on your team and end up having a profound impact on the outcome of the project—and sometimes even save lives! So, listen to your folks and truly believe: If you take care of your people, they will take care of you.

THE STRATEGY

So, how do you take care of your mentee? Here are five strategies I use when entering a new mentor-mentee relationship: make connections, walk with your mentee, have intentional conversations, seek feedback, and achieve *swing*.

MAKE CONNECTIONS

During my first meeting with my mentee, I try to make a connection by telling my story and then inviting the mentee to tell their story. A lot of my story is my professional journey, but I also include some personal challenges and joys.

On the professional front, I begin with my career passions, the *why* I pursued what I pursued. I began my career designing and building structures, then evolved to designing and building teams and organizations. My story includes twists and turns in the journey, some successes, and some failures. Oftentimes, sharing failures and vulnerabilities makes for a deeper and quicker connection to my mentee, who might be experiencing similar challenges.

On the personal front, my story always includes being widowed in my 30s and going through a very challenging and dark time. But, with perseverance and a lot of help from family and friends getting me through the rough spots, I met and married my current wife, who was also widowed in her 30s. Talk about a way to connect! That's a story for another book.

Another way I try to build a relationship with my mentee quickly is by inviting them to my home, if we live in the same region. I believe meeting at my home and sitting out on my porch shows an intent to consider them like family. It also offers a chance to introduce them to my wife, who also mentors for the Severn Leadership Group.

The goal is to build a trusting relationship. Be driven by a quote attributed to Theodore Roosevelt: "Nobody cares how much you know, until they know how much you care."

WALK WITH YOUR MENTEE

I find that the most difficult challenge in mentoring is listening to some problem the mentee is having and resisting the urge to jump in and fix it for them. I'm thinking, *I've had this problem before, and I know exactly how to fix it. Just do this...* It's a natural response to someone you care about.

I have the same temptation with my daughters. Sometimes jumping in there is the right thing to do: "Dad, how do you change a tire?" But when it's a more complex situation—"Dad, I have this challenging colleague at work who I need for support with my proposal"—a different response is called for. As a mentor, to have a lasting impact, you need not fix it for them, but walk beside them, listen, ask questions, and let them discover the solution.

In our mentor certification process for the Severn Leadership Group program, we hammer on this principle: *A mentor is not someone who walks ahead to show you how they did it. A mentor walks alongside you to show you what you can do.* Easier said than done.

There's no higher gratification from being a mentor than to see your mentee work through an issue (with a little help and encouragement) and develop a plan. Then, it's their plan, not my plan. They own it! Plus, you, as the mentor, learn so much yourself.

HAVE INTENTIONAL CONVERSATIONS

One of the most important lessons I've learned along the way is that in almost any conversation you have, both at work and at home, you're either *enrolling* or *disenrolling* someone into something. Intentionally or not, you're either pulling someone towards you or an idea, or pushing someone away from you or an idea. Think about it.

I was working in Jakarta, Indonesia, with my team. We were immersed in some intense negotiations with our partners. I brought in an outside consultant to work with us to develop strategies to build relationships with our partners. During those discussions, the consultant introduced the concept that most of our conversations involve either enrolling or disenrolling our audience.

We were in the middle of this discussion when one of my teammates cried out, like a bolt of lightning had hit him, "That's what's going on!"

He went on to say, "I've gone home each night, complaining to my wife about how difficult my job is here. Last night, she said, 'Let's pack up the kids and go back home to the States; this isn't worth it!'"

His wife had put her career on hold, pulled their kids out of school, and moved to Jakarta to support his career, and all she heard was him complaining about his job. "Why are we doing this?" she asked. It wasn't his intent at all to suggest a move back to the States. He liked much of his job, but was unloading the bad and ugly on his wife.

I challenge you to consider how you engage with your mentee, teammate, or spouse. Are you enrolling or disenrolling? I still catch myself expressing disenrolling thoughts when I have no intention of doing so.

SEEK FEEDBACK

An essential element for self-improvement and achieving excellence is seeking feedback in any endeavor. It exposes your blind spots and builds trust with those providing the feedback.

Throughout my career, when I conducted one-on-one counseling sessions with my employees, I ended with the question, "What can I do better to help you and our team?" It opens the door for feedback and shows I value their advice.

In addition, my company introduced a formal 360-degree feedback process whereby I solicited feedback from not only my manager but also my peers and direct reports. My direct reports identified that my top area for improvement was to give more explicit recognition more often to individuals for jobs well done. My initial reaction: *They were just doing their jobs, doing what they got paid to do.* Admittedly old school, but in my defense, that's the school I had attended.

Throughout my career, I've tried to develop a sense of caring for my teammates and encourage caring between their teammates. I hopefully demonstrated it through my actions and behaviors, but I didn't always express it in words. Although I cared about them, I wasn't expressing it effectively. For whatever reason, it never came naturally to me to verbalize recognition.

In response to the feedback, I gathered my team. "Your feedback on recognition is fair; it has never come naturally to me. Help me. What can I do to fix it?"

We came up with a process of adding an agenda item to my weekly Friday morning staff meeting, in which I solicited nominees who deserved special recognition for extraordinary work effort. Then, on Friday afternoon, I carved out some time to stop by their office in person, write a thank-you note, send an email halfway around the world, or award a dinner for them and their families to express my gratitude for a job well done.

Boy, it was a win-win proposition! The recipients were very appreciative of the recognition and oftentimes commented, "I was just doing my job." I felt so good for having reached out to them. What a great way to end the week!

ACHIEVE *SWING*

In the sport of rowing, *swing* is the point when a nine-person crew is in perfect harmony, resulting in extraordinary boat speed, way beyond the expected sum of its parts. This phenomenon is best captured in Daniel James Brown's book, *Boys in the Boat*, which tells the true story of the University of Washington's rowing team journeying together to win the gold medal in the 1936 Berlin Olympics, against all odds. Essential elements of achieving swing are the love and relationships of the coach, team members, and a very wise boat builder.

I haven't rowed on a team before, but I've played on a lot of football, baseball, and basketball teams over the years, and I've experienced swing on a number of those teams. In all cases, on the teams in which swing was achieved, there was a leader—usually the coach, but sometimes a team member—who cared deeply about the players and inspired them to care about each other. On those teams, as a player, I, first and foremost, was driven not to disappoint my coach, nor my other teammates. These kinds of relationships aren't the only thing you need to achieve swing, but they're essential. It's the magic of achieving extraordinary performance and results.

In my career, I've also achieved swing working with certain teams at certain times. Although I didn't necessarily always have the A-list players, we achieved extraordinary results through a deep caring for our fellow teammates.

In Sig Berg's book, *The Virtue Proposition: Five Virtues That Will Transform Leadership, Team Performance, and You*, two of the transcendental virtues discussed in the book—and anchoring the Severn Leadership Group's training program—are love and relationships. To better understand these virtues in the context of business, we encourage a self-assessment, whereby you rate yourself on the following behaviors:

For love,

- I serve others before myself
- I seek to inspire others
- I aim to build the capacity of others
- I believe in my team
- I display empathy and compassion
- I treat others with respect
- I listen
- I ask questions
- I can be tough or challenging when necessary
- I do not humiliate another person, group, or adversary

For relationships,

- I recognize that leadership is about people, not things
- I know my people
- I care about my people
- I encourage my people
- I teach my people
- I provide constructive feedback
- I focus on people, not my career
- I build trust
- I am approachable

For each behavior, rate yourself on a scale of one to five from *rarely performing* to *consistently performing* those behaviors. Where do you stand with your team?

SUMMARY

I've tried to show the need to win the hearts and minds of those whom you mentor and lead by developing caring relationships. These kinds of relationships are not the only thing you need to achieve swing, but they're essential to achieving extraordinary performance and results. I've highlighted some of the tools I have used. Bottom line: Take care of your people and they will take care of you.

Ray L. Steinmetz is currently a volunteer and certified mentor for the Severn Leadership Group (SLG), having served on its board of directors for many years. SLG is a nonprofit organization dedicated to developing leaders of character and purpose, committed to serving others before self.

Ray had a successful and rewarding 36-year career in the energy industry. He held numerous project management leadership positions at ExxonMobil in various locations around the world. The teams Ray led were responsible for the planning, design, construction, and start-up of energy facilities. His projects ranged in scope, from several hundred million to several billions of dollars in investments.

His teams were recognized for their execution excellence and extraordinary safety performance. He also worked directly with host governments to build relationships with their national energy companies. Ray ultimately became responsible for ExxonMobil's Production Company (EMPC) projects worldwide, where he led a functional organization to provide support and grow functional excellence for EMPC's global project portfolio.

Ray graduated from Swarthmore College with a bachelor's degree with Distinction in Engineering in 1974 and from Princeton University with a master's degree in Structural Engineering in 1976. Ray completed executive leadership courses at Columbia Business School, UNC's Kenan-Flagler Business School, and Thunderbird's American Graduate School of International Management.

Ray and his wife, Torri Corcoran, live in Annapolis, Maryland. They have two spirited daughters and an outstanding son-in-law, now living in Oregon and NYC. Ray and his family had the opportunity to live overseas in Indonesia, England, and Malaysia. His interests include boating, hiking, golfing, traveling, and spending time with family and friends.

Connect with Ray:

Email: ray.steinmetz@severnleadership.org

LinkedIn: https://www.linkedin.com/in/ray-steinmetz-98144b78

CHAPTER TWENTY

BE A HEAD-AND HEART-BASED MENTOR

INCREASE IMPACT WITH EMOTIONAL AWARENESS

Loralei Matisse

The greatest challenge in life is to be our own person and accept that being different is a blessing and not a curse. A person who knows who they are lives a simple life by eliminating from their orbit anything that does not align with his or her overriding purpose and values.

~ Kilroy J. Oldster, *Dead Toad Scrolls*

"I'm going to get you to think differently. You need to know I'm going to push you to make some transformations you weren't expecting. I need to know if you're willing to be truly uncomfortable."

Sitting in the Tampa International Airport terminal waiting for my plane to board, the mentee on the other end paused. Military trained. High-level assignments. Excelling at tactical systems and strategy, which, at the time of our call, had saved hundreds of lives. A potential mentee who could figure out mathematical equations off the top of his head. His skills and leadership experience could easily overshadow mine.

With the noise and bustle of the airport, people rushing to planes, and people ordering coffee and food, I sat secluded, waiting. Waiting not only for boarding assignments to be called but also for this mentee to decide if this was going to work or not.

In all honesty, I wasn't attached to his answer.

"Yes."

The answer was enthusiastic and resounding over the phone, and immediately, I questioned it. Doubt rushing in, I wondered if the answer was rote and swift based on his training, or if it was authentically courageous.

What quieted the doubt was remembering his request to be paired with a mentor unlike himself. Someone non-military. Someone who would challenge him to get out of his way.

Will he let me push him from his head knowledge and into his heart? Or will he fight me and stay in his battleground state of mind?

Eagerness to tackle this challenge started a shift in me.

We'd soon find out.

MY STORY

I was angry. Extraordinarily angry.

Words escaped me because the fury inside came to a boiling point. I could breathe fire if I opened my mouth. Everything felt overwhelming, but I had no idea why.

Anger got me fired. Anger got me disciplined. Anger almost ruined any type of future I had. And although anger was the most volatile emotion, it wasn't the only one I didn't know how to identify or use at the right time. *I want to kill this person right now. And I don't look good in federal orange.*

Growing up, I never really knew what it felt like to be authentically happy, and if I'm really honest, sad or loving. Most times, I was angry or numb. Feelings, let alone emotions, weren't a good thing growing up. I couldn't identify how I felt. Nor did I know how to regulate or use it for good.

If you asked me how I was, I'd say fine. It was the only answer I knew.

Fine. Even when I wasn't.

In addition to the emotional immaturity, I naturally possess an inherited quality of overthinking. *Thanks, Mom. Worst-case scenarios with multiple contingency plans. Contingency plans with contingency plans.* It's one of my best traits, *and also my most challenging.* Always preparing for the shoe to drop, I come up with every possible scenario and have a plan to survive pretty much all of it.

However, one plan I couldn't seem to get right concerned the story of not being worthy, *or even smart enough* to be in rooms with some of the influential people I surrounded myself with. Everyone else deserved the spotlight more than I did. My job was to make them look good, like a good stage manager making the star of the show shine. *I'm the person in black working behind the scenes, invisible.*

Not the greatest example of a mentor to learn techniques from, right? You want someone courageous, strong, who can lead you through hell. Not someone fading into the background.

This story spun its way through my childhood, teen years, and even into adulthood, tripping me up every chance I had to come out from the shadows into a spotlight of my own. *Very likely a deep cause of my anger.*

One of the last times I experienced this story was in 2020. The world shut down. All of us were inside reflecting on the state of the world, what was important in our lives, and what we wanted for our future. At the time, I was on a trajectory to become either an executive director of a nonprofit or finally make the jump into the legislative and political world. Both paths fueled my desire to make an impact, create change, and leave a legacy.

Now, to give a bit more color to this story, I moved across the country from Colorado to St. Petersburg, Florida, by myself. My dog and I. No family. No direction. No job. No community. The only thing driving this insane idea was a woo-woo plan that had me following some kind of pull to be here.

What was I thinking moving all the way here, thinking I'd become an author, make a difference, find the one I'd spend the rest of my life with, and be able to travel the world? You thought you'd drive right into the driveway of a perfect life? What?!?!

Idealist, right?

We all have plans for our future. Yet somehow, the Universe or God or whatever you believe in sometimes has something quite different in mind. And that's usually some form of using the talents and quirks we've hidden because they didn't fit into the "normal" way of doing business, life, or love.

ONE LAST TIME

To move my executive director dream forward, I enrolled in some professional training and personal growth programs. These came exactly when I was willing to go to the next level. Much like the overused quote of the teacher appearing, I was ready.

The professional training was a leadership development course based on love, integrity, and relationships. *I didn't need another leadership course;* however, if being a true community leader was the goal, it would be better to have additional training rather than come in with what I already knew.

Virtual training was a new thing back in early 2020. As we sat in our respective squares online in our first session, we began with introductions. Here again, I found myself surrounded by people of influence, FBI agents, nonprofit fundraisers raising millions, military strategists, fighter pilots, and industry leaders—each from the upper East Coast of the U.S. and personally invited to participate in this first-of-its-kind training.

Right on cue, the old familiar story, along with all the feelings and emotions. *Why am I part of this group?* Immediate comparison. No other real-life experience would have brought this level of experience or expertise. *Why am I even here?*

But something about this journey was different.

For nine months, each week, something new awakened in me. How I thought internally was stripped away. Habits, beliefs, emotions, and understanding my values recreated me from the inside out. Raw, bare, vulnerable. I cried in front of these people. Shared fears I thought would never be verbalized were brought into light.

Pushed to the far edges of the comfort zones I created to keep me safe, I found something powerful and lasting. I would no longer be the same person who signed up for the course.

Now, this was not the first time I'd been rocked by a training. It's happened several times with therapy, recovery, spiritual transformational programs, and inner child work led by teachers and mentors like Sherri, Terry, Bhajan, Roger, Cynthia, and others. Rigorous programs diving deep into who you are, reflecting on personal experiences, and how we're formed. I became increasingly aware of bad habits and patterns. *I'd created some awful ones that damaged me and several others along the way.*

In all of these, I'd work on emotions. *So many emotions.* But something was still missing.

The one thing absent in all of them was emotional intelligence, and what a gift; it was part of this leadership course. The language of emotions, self-awareness, and regard gave me a vocabulary. It made everything I'd ever learned before finally make sense. *I want to use this every day—be fluent and teach others.*

KNOW THYSELF

When awareness is brought to an emotion, power is brought to your life.

~ Tara Meyer Robson

The game changed. All the talents and skills I used in the background for others were finally ready to come forward as tools to coach and mentor. No longer did I feel unworthy to be in rooms. Many times, I was invited specifically for the way I showed up. I led differently. Mentored differently.

Different is my superpower.

I'm a feeling person, always asking you to tap into the feeling part, your gut, your intuition. Emotions are powerful, as important as skills and business knowledge. It was part of the secret of strong, approachable leaders, creating exceptional teams, empowering individuals, and making lasting change.

But emotions don't belong in business, do they? I believe they do.

How could I use them and this new language to create that transformational change?

Well, let's head back to the mentee call from the beginning.

Remember, high-level military, strategic, and very heady.

My first mentee call was a failure. No one died, but it contained enough miscommunication that I wondered if we'd ever get on the same page *or they'd ask for another mentor ASAP.*

Oh crap. I don't speak military. Don't understand it. I'm not getting through.

I've lived by the example of not needing to know everything. I just need to know who knows it and how fast I can get to them. With that in mind, I immediately contacted some fellow mentors within the armed forces to give me guidance on speaking their language so that mentoring sessions would have the greatest impact.

He's talking at such a high level, I'm not sure I can get him to slow down to even hear me. He's speaking with four-star generals daily. How do I get through to him?

With a bit more knowledge and tactical language I brought into our session, emotions and feelings were easier to discuss, and I could provide key ways to reframe and broaden his military situational myopic vision.

One of the main things we worked on was choosing a new career path. He was leaving the military. *The only thing he'd ever known. How would we change the way he viewed the world and his future, without the military?* We started by listening and getting radically curious about his passions, values, and outside interests. We uncovered old passions and skills he couldn't use in his day-to-day commands that lit up his heart. By stretching and reaching and getting quiet, he enthusiastically tapped into his path.

You don't need to have all the answers. You just need to be willing to see the possibilities differently.

Equally impressive, his emotions came out to play more often. He spoke more slowly and thoughtfully. He paused a bit more to take in the full weight of his decisions instead of giving rote answers. His head started speaking to his heart instead of it being the dominant force.

Our last mentoring session was extraordinary. I could hear the excitement in his voice as he came online. He was like a little kid who'd found all the presents and could barely wait to share all the joy.

His demeanor changed; he was inviting and engaging. Selfless. He laughed at himself more often. He spoke of love when he saw his next career move. He even mentored another person who wanted a similar career change.

A bit after our last call, I received a text.

'I must say you are incredibly wise... I am reaching out to tell you I accepted a job offer to fast-track [for a finance job]. It came to fruition in the short time between our last call and now. Thank you so much for your advice, wisdom, counsel, and kindness. You are amazing, and I could not have done this without you. I can't believe it happened. It is unfathomable that this was a possibility. I cannot thank you enough for how much of a difference your mentorship and encouragement made.'

When I spoke to him months later, he was loving what he was doing, listening more actively, using his gut more often, and staying curious in his relationships with others.

Recalling our airport conversation, this wasn't the same person who used his "wins" to impress. He was now a well-rounded person, relating to others differently.

Was this a fluke? Or did becoming fluent in his language, using love, virtues, and curiosity, open doors people would be willing to walk through (*even if it did seem a bit woo-woo*)?

All I know, based on these and other experiences, is that the first rule of business applies. Find ways to serve people and improve others' lives over profits, and you'll succeed every time.

THE STRATEGY

I'm a big believer in testing things out. See if they work. Adapt them for your use. Use one and leave the rest. Not everything works for every mentee or mentor.

Life is an experiment. Get into the lab and see what happens. I invite you to check them out for yourself. Add one or all of these strategies to your growing toolbox. May they help you show up fully to whomever is in front of you at this moment (mentee, employee, or any other relationship).

We're all on the journey together, learning and growing in the role of both leader and follower.

LEARN THEIR LANGUAGE

Mentors are full of knowledge. That's why individuals gravitate to us or not. We usually have what they want in their life, and we can, more often than not, move them to the next level. However, no matter how good your mentoring, what good is it if they don't understand you?

I heard once from a mentor, "It doesn't matter what you have to teach if no one comprehends what you say."

Do you speak the same language as your mentee? If not, begin with the following:

- How best do you learn? Listen? Understand?
  - Auditory? Kinesthetic? Verbal?

- Understand their background, because language matters.
  - Corporate versus military versus nonprofit.

- What's their family and relationship background?
  - Their language, environment, and place in the family dynamic factor greatly into comprehension.

- How do they express emotions? Get familiar with how it shows up.
  - No expressions to OMG over-the-top.

UNCONDITIONAL ACTIVE LISTENING

The art of active listening is being fully present with someone. Most of us are hopefully familiar with this definition. Now, let's add unconditional to active listening. How does it change this already engaged action? What exactly do I mean by unconditional active listening?

As humans, we come with biases. They appear at the most inconvenient times, and in many cases, taint the way we speak or show up as leaders. Unconditional active listening is the act of questioning your own biases while being an active listener.

A mentee comes to you for guidance, wisdom, foresight, and direction. However, some mentors I've had and others I've witnessed make mentoring all about them. It's not. One of the most impactful things a mentor can do is hold their tongue while actively listening.

- Listening actively is an intentional act.

  ○ Choose to remove all other distractions.

- Mentoring isn't about you pouring your wisdom into someone else. It's listening, questioning, and using experience and guidance to move someone else forward in the direction of their dreams, goals, and outcomes.

  ○ Remove yourself from the equation. Their experience is as important as yours.

  ○ Stay open by listening without the need to speak. Sometimes the mentee needs to talk something out without input. Let them. Don't assume they are looking for a solution. Ask them.

- As you listen, and if a bias or judgment comes forward, question it.

  ○ Example: If you have a bias on a specific type of job, ask yourself, "Can I remove this idea from this conversation?" You can always return to your bias afterward.

RADICAL CURIOSITY

Today, we find books about radical acceptance and radical forgiveness—ways to help us let things go and accept where our lives and experiences have brought us. It also allows us to learn tools and ways to remove those things and ideas that weigh us down.

Radical curiosity is one where you dig deeper than you think possible. Over the years in my work, I've honed skills to listen to what isn't being said, what's being skirted around, and even to the speaking tone. When one of these pings for me, I feel like a detective searching for clues of an underlying value, idea, belief, or feeling driving this individual.

Now, mentor time isn't therapy time (though sometimes it can be). You don't need to dig like a therapist. However, when you build trust with your mentee, you can push a little further and dig into whys, hows, and "Are you sure?" more easily.

I find the following helpful:

- What if?

  ○ What if you find yourself without this position in two months? Will the decision you make now matter?

  ○ What if the outcome is more horrific (or even better) than you planned for? What then?

  ○ What if you could choose something else? What would it be?

- Tap into the feelings.

  ○ Breathe into the experience as if it had already occurred. What do you feel?

- So what?

  ○ Use this one to dive into a situation you want to break through. The idea is that each time you ask, you uncover other factors you may not have considered. It creates tension and allows for more creativity.

- Are you complete?

  o I find this one question helpful when something hasn't yet been said, or someone hasn't quite accessed the courage to share something vulnerable. Using this question creates an intentional pause and space for psychological safety, allowing the other person to check in with themselves. This one is a great tool for having the other person be fully seen, heard, and encouraged.

BRING THE WOO-WOO

Yes, I said it. Woo-woo. Woo-woo as in spiritual, unexplainable phenomena, and other ways people believe that may not fit into the "norm." Finding out values, practices, or what your mentee believes or doesn't believe can be used as fodder to drive the conversation, especially when someone gets stuck.

Please note: You don't have to believe the same. You have to know if they do or not.

Here's how I invite the conversation:

- Tell me about your belief system.
- Where do you find yourself walking away from or leaning into your beliefs?
- What are the virtues you live by? Which one is the strongest, and how does it appear in your daily life?

Always remember: Your mentee is a whole person—mental, physical, spiritual, and emotional. Treat them as such, and you may find, by using the tools above, that you gain a larger view of who they are, what motivates them, and how you can show up even better as a guiding force.

Feel free to drop me a line and tell me how any of these tools worked for you and your mentee. I always look forward to hearing from others on their growth journeys.

Loralei Matisse is an author, SLG program manager for virtual cohorts, emotional intelligence facilitator and coach, and religious science practitioner. In her past lives, she's been a small business owner, lobbyist liaison, chief of staff, project and operations manager in fields of university education, nonprofit capacity training, grant writing, and private equity.

As a founding member and leader within many nonprofits, she leads from a place of passion for building strong foundations rather than bridges by having courageous conversations. As a mentor, her skills at inviting the uncomfortable into conversation and using active listening and radical curiosity to change perceptions help individuals courageously create actionable ways to live all-in, using head and heart in all areas of their lives.

Understanding the interconnection between heart and mind and using spiritual as well as leadership tools, Loralei has helped many transform their lives, expanding their awareness of self, the greater community, and all the ways they can be more balanced in the face of any type of change.

Loralei lives in St. Petersburg, Florida, with her two dogs Raya and Remy, and fills her spare time being the go-to beta reader for leadership development books.

If you're ready to do it differently, contact Loralei to schedule an EQ assessment, coaching, or one-on-one mentoring.

Connect with Loralei:

Email: EQLoralei@gmail.com

CHAPTER TWENTY-ONE

ELEVATED MENTORING

GUARANTEED POSITIVE CONSEQUENCES FOR LEADERS

Bruce Engelhardt, Executive Coach (CEC)

Nobody cares how much you know, until they know how much you care.

~ Theodore Roosevelt

Effective leadership is not about making speeches or being liked; leadership is defined by results, not attributes.

~ Peter Drucker

Picture a coin, which, when used, will enable you to elevate your mentoring to a new level, guaranteeing positive outcomes for the mentored leader. On one side of the coin is the word "care," and on the other side is the word "results." If the coin is blank on either side, it is counterfeit and will not buy anything. How do you mint this mentoring coin? This chapter is about how to use these two primary focus points in your mentoring.

MY STORY

I can't believe I'm going toe-to-toe with the CEO.

During the interview process for my first job, the CEO gave me some tasks to carry out before I began working full-time for him. The tasks involved senior-year college academic performance. I did what he told me halfheartedly because the tasks seemed silly to me. Now, I had been on the job for three years. I was proud of all I did in my first years as a junior engineer.

It was time to go to headquarters and pass my senior engineer examination. I did so with excellent results. However, the CEO called me in to "discuss my progress."

He started out with, "Why didn't you do what I told you to do in your senior year?"

Stunned, I bravely answered, "Sir, I did do what you told me to do. I got a 4.0 in physics my first semester and a 3.3 my second semester."

We argued back and forth. *Somehow, he's making me tell him my truth. In fact, he demands it.*

When I finished justifying myself and making excuses, he said, in so many words, "You completed the letter of what I asked for, but didn't give me what I wanted."

I was clueless. *What does he mean? Why is he challenging me after all the work I put in?*

Finally, he asked, "Did you do your very best?"

I knew the answer deep down. I said, "No, I did not." That was the end of the conversation.

Afterward, I felt puzzled. This was before the concept of emotional intelligence, and the CEO's style was abrupt and off-putting. However, I eventually came to see he was right. Mostly, after this conversation, I was determined to change.

I never again want to answer that question with anything but, "Yes, I did my very best."

The CEO mentor gave me all I could have asked for in one short conversation. He showed me he cared about me. He turned his critique into a means for me to get better future results by defining terms so we both knew we were talking about the same thing. He spoke the truth. And the truth was, my effort was good, but not my best. At the end of the conversation, he asked me a probing question which was a stimulus for personal change. He got my attention!

THE STRATEGY

SHOW CARE

How did the mentor in my story show care? He didn't ask me about my family, my hobbies, or my favorite books. This is what he did: Firstly, he was the big boss, the CEO—extraordinarily busy, yet he gave me his undivided attention and time. Secondly, he listened to me—even my excuses. Thirdly, he provided me with honest feedback.

Most importantly, he treated me as an intellectual equal. His intense honesty and probing demeanor showed me he cared deeply about the work we were doing, and that my role *mattered*. He created an atmosphere of authenticity. He stayed focused, not on the details of my senior year academic performance. Instead, he was after more. He wanted to know about my inner character, about my core. Did I give it my best shot? This is the ultimate way to show someone you care—by caring about their inner character.

There are some lessons for mentors here. Showing care can take on many behaviors. People can show they care by being vulnerable, being honest and authentic, deep listening, giving of their time, valuing the mentored leader, and more. All these behaviors are valid. But, in my experience, the heart of showing care has to do with three primary themes, which are inclusive:

1. **Valuing the mentored leader,** treating them as a valued team member whose contribution matters to you.

2. **Giving the mentored leader your undivided time.** This doesn't mean wasting time; it means making every moment count. Sometimes a silent pause is the best way to make a moment count!

3. **Being truly authentic,** which may mean showing the vulnerability to recount your own challenges and failures. This can take the form of intense, honest feedback like I received from my CEO mentor. The mentor showed me he cared by giving me intensely honest feedback. I may not have appreciated the feedback at the time, but later? Yes!

Showing care can take time, especially if there's broken trust involved. Intensely honest feedback may not be the place to start in a new relationship. People can sense whether you are being truly honest with them. And they crave honesty.

As a mentor, I have found that being truly authentic and humble helps break down any barriers that exist. It's not easy to be vulnerable because it opens us up to judgment and even rejection. So, this step involves risking rejection and disapproval. In the end, showing care is about building trust. The first side of the coin needs to be the first step for both mentor and mentee. We might call this the prerequisite or foundation for mentoring and leading. Showing care is a prerequisite, but it is also a continuous foundation, never-ending.

Leadership guru John C. Maxwell puts it like this: "Character makes trust possible, and trust is the foundation of leadership." When we practice elevated mentorship, we use character—the five virtues found in Sig Berg's book, *The Value Proposition*. These virtues are love, integrity, truth, excellence, and relationships. When we use these virtues to make trust possible, we end up concurrently modeling elevated leadership and mentorship.

GETTING RESULTS

Results are the other side of the mentoring coin. Some would define pure executive coaching as asking probing questions in a way that enables the leader to solve their own challenges. It can also be a useful concept in mentoring.

However, I think mentoring can and does involve more. Mentorship is a longer-term relationship. It can be less transactional than coaching.

Elevated mentoring involves imparting the mentor's wisdom and experience, especially if the leader works on your team.

How can this work? I see the getting results part of mentoring as having three stages:

1. Defining terminology.

2. Establishing truths.

3. Asking probing questions to evoke change.

In the story above, the mentor used all three of these stages:

- **He defined terms.** In my lexicon, "I did what you told me to do." But his desire went beyond the specifics of the project. I did what I needed to get by. He wanted me to do "my very best." If I had been more thoughtful, I could have surmised this truth from the beginning.

- **He established truth.** By asking the question, "Did you do your very best?" I could have played word games and asked, "What is my best?" or even, "Who says doing my best is my truth?" But I am not a relativist. My truth is I always want to do my best, and the mentor sensed this.

- **His question stage had another purpose.** It probed deep and challenged me to look past this one project. The other question I heard in my head was, "Will you do your best in the future?" Mentors are wise to avoid yes/no questions and use open-ended questions instead. At first, the question my mentor asked me appears to be a yes/no question. But the implied question was, "What's your plan for doing your best from now on?" or "What does a commitment to excellence look like for you?" These implied questions caused me to change my life in profound ways.

This three-stage approach does so much. It ensures the mentor and mentee are not talking past each other; they have common definitions and understanding of the subject at hand. It provides a method for the mentor to insert truth, wisdom, and experience that the mentee doesn't have.

As a warning, the mentor should avoid inserting wisdom and experience in a directive manner. "What works for me" or "I find the following to be an effective approach" are better. *What if the leader works as a member of your team?* Ideally, the mentee will pick up on your wisdom and draw up an action plan without you asking. If not, query them, "As a result of our time together, what is your action plan?" If they still don't come close to a workable solution, ask them to work on it and then schedule a follow-up session. If you end up giving orders and specific direction, you will have moved from mentor to boss. Not ideal for the long term, however, this outcome is better than taking a purely directive approach from the beginning of your session. And it is better than ambiguity- you don't want your mentee leaving confused.

Finally, in the third stage, the probing question puts the ball in the aspiring leader's court by making the discussion about them personally.

MENTORING CHALLENGES

Let's consider some real-life mentoring challenges.

- **Time management.** "Virtue-based leadership needs time. How will I ever find the time for it?"

    ○ **Defining terms.** Here we try to define current time demands. A time log might be a beneficial exercise, as well as looking at a typical daily schedule, trying to specifically define current time use.

    ○ **Establishing truths.** My experience and wisdom led the mentored leader to the Eisenhower time management matrix, espoused by President Dwight Eisenhower and later Stephen Covey in his book, *The 7 Habits of Highly Effective People.* The four-quadrant matrix consists of: 1. Important/Not Urgent; 2. Important/Urgent; 3. Not Important/Urgent and 4. Not Important/ Not Urgent. The key here is to maximize your time spent in the number one quadrant, thereby spending time on important tasks before they become urgent. The other rule is to spend **no** time in the time-wasting number 4 quadrant.

    ○ **Probing questions.** Which quadrant do you spend your time in? What time-wasting tasks are you doing? If you spent more time on virtuous and emotionally intelligent leadership, what would you spend less time on?

- **Motivation.** "How can I motivate and inspire my team to take it to the next level?"

  ○ **Defining terms.** Encourage your mentee to assign metrics to describe their team's motivation level. Using these metrics, the leader can figure out what team engagement or motivation level is now. Also, define engagement goals: where you want them to be. Without metrics, you can't make progress. Find ways to measure your team's inspiration level, motivation, and engagement. This is no easy task, and every team and team leader are different. A well-executed 360 evaluation or survey might be the answer if used properly. Walking around the workplace, either physically or virtually, and then assigning a numerical score can be effective if done every day.

  ○ **Establishing truths.** In this example, the metrics chosen will go a long way toward guiding the mentor to share her wisdom and experience. Short examples and stories are gold here, but they must be pithy. In my experience, when you are changing a team's culture, the team leader models the desired behavior in everything she does. This means if you want your team to be motivated, you must show them your own motivation. If you want them to be enthusiastic, you must model enthusiasm. Once they start emulating you, the culture will change like a geometric progression. It only takes one follower to get the change moving. Changing culture is a "retail" proposition. Writing long policy statements for everyone to ponder or even ignore rarely works. The audience wonders, "What does this mean? Is it another front-office daydream?" Changing culture happens one interaction at a time.

  ○ **Probing questions.** What are your chosen metrics to look at team engagement and culture? What, specifically, will you do to model the desired behaviors for your team?

Leadership means forming a team and working toward common objectives that are tied to time, metrics, and resources.

~ Russel Honore

- **Micromanagement, accountability, and feedback.** "My team thinks I'm a micromanager, but all I want is for them to do their jobs. How do I hold them accountable in a positive way? Feedback has a negative connotation; what should I do?"

  ○ **Defining terms.** For this challenge, defining terms for yourself and the team is critically important. For example, micromanagement is a management style where a manager closely observes, supervises, and/or controls their employees' work. People who micromanage immerse themselves in others' work. But asking for periodic progress reports is not micromanagement. Giving specific feedback, which focuses on a specific occasion and the specific behavior of a team member, is not micromanagement. This is especially true if the leader asks the team member what their intent was on this occasion. Clarifying how you intend to check progress and give feedback up front is the ideal scenario. Defining feedback not as criticism, but as a means of continuous improvement, is also a first step.

  ○ **Establishing truths.** Actions speak louder than words in this sensitive challenge area. Saying one thing and doing another can sabotage the best of good intentions. This happens when deadlines are looming, and the pressure is on. The golden rule in the case of deadlines and pressure from the top is the adage–P7: "Proper previous planning prevents pretty poor performance." Now we may be back in the time management challenge. Are you spending enough time in the important/not urgent quadrant? The other important truth here is that leaders need to train their teams. John Wooden, champion UCLA basketball coach, put it this way: "If you don't have time to do it right in the first place, how will you ever find time to do it over?" Doing it right the first time requires team training and evaluation.

  ○ **Probing questions.** What is your plan to communicate your accountability and feedback process with your team? What are you doing to guide their expectations about micromanagement? What is your plan to set up a culture of continuous improvement? What will you do to focus on the five virtues mentioned above and your own emotional intelligence toward these challenges? What's your attitude toward receiving feedback for yourself? How does your process encourage constructive ideas for change and discourage personal attacks?

BOTTOM LINE

Elevated mentoring is like a coin with care on one side and results on the other. These two focus areas work together to get guaranteed positive consequences for mentors and leaders. You cannot focus on one without the other.

All the caring in the world without a results focus will end with disappointment. A results focus without caring, similarly, will be devoid of trust and won't bring long-term success. So, we start with the virtues to build trust; this is a continuous process. Once we prove a modicum of trust, we look at mentoring for results through the lens of defining terms, establishing truth, and asking probing questions. This is elevated mentoring.

Bruce Engelhardt, Executive Coach (CEC), is the CEO of Flagship Coaching LLC. He is an experienced mentor and board member for the Severn Leadership Group. Previously, he spent 15 years as CEO of a two-billion-dollar financial services nonprofit. He has served on several boards, including managing trustee for Fincantieri's USA Marine Trust and board first vice chair at Navy Federal Credit Union.

Bruce is a graduate of the Center for Executive Coaching, was a fellow at Harvard University's John F. Kennedy School of Government, has a M.S. from the University of Southern California, and a B.S. in physics from the U.S. Naval Academy. He's passionate about virtue-based leadership and, in his free time, is committed to endurance bicycling and playing the saxophone.

Connect with Bruce:

LinkedIn: https://www.linkedin.com/in/engelharbb677

Email: flagshipcoaching@gmail.com

CHAPTER TWENTY-TWO

EMPATHETIC ACCOUNTABILITY

SHARED COMMITMENTS FROM RELATIONSHIPS OF TRUST

CDR James B. Montgomery, U.S.Navy

We often see accountability as the negative consequence of failing to complete a task. Merriam-Webster defines accountability as "an obligation or willingness to accept responsibility or account for one's actions[1]." This notion of accounting for one's actions suggests there is another individual responsible for holding the allegedly guilty party accountable. This limited view of accountability frequently results in negative interactions and misses the genuine opportunities positive accountability presents.

As an officer in the United States Submarine Force, I learned throughout my career to adjust how I hold my Sailors accountable. My leadership and mentorship growth resulted from altering my interactions following failures and feedback. In my story, I contrast an example of personal failure with the success that emerged from change. My tool applies this learning to the mentor-mentee relationship, ensuring the mentee achieves their desired personal growth.

---

1 Merriam-Webster. "Accountability." Definition of Accountability, 1 June 2025, www.merriam-webster.com/dictionary/accountability.

MY STORY

Empathetic accountability from mentor to mentee leverages relationships of trust to promote personal growth.

In January 2018, I relieved as the engineer officer on the USS Alaska (SSBN 732) (Gold), an Ohio-class ballistic missile submarine. In this role, I was responsible for leading and training my sixty Sailor department of engineering professionals in the operations and maintenance of the nuclear propulsion plant and its supporting engineering equipment.

In April, we got the ship underway to execute a strategic deterrent patrol. During this patrol, our ship was scheduled for a fleet commander's engineering inspection at the end of May, to ensure my department was operating the propulsion plant to the correct standards. One of the key elements of this inspection is assessing my department's ability to respond to any material failure that may occur. To prepare for this assessment, and more importantly, to ensure our readiness to operate our ship, we routinely conducted engineering drills. My example of personal failure occurred during one of these drills.

THE FAILURE

We were halfway through a fire drill involving a simulated electric motor controller fire that spread to the engine room's outboard section. The fire was out. The engineering officer of the watch, or EOOW, worked on his plan to restore the engine room to full operation. I was in the maneuvering area where the EOOW stood watch to observe and assess his performance.

The EOOW stared at the pages of his technical manuals, searching for an answer he wasn't going to find. After several minutes of doing nothing, he whispered to the room, "Attention to maneuvering for a brief."

No one responded.

Why is he being so quiet?

I attempted to prompt him. "EOOW, you need to be louder if you want your team to hear you. No one understood what you just said."

"Attention to maneuvering for brief." The EOOW only barely increased the volume of his voice. His shoulders slumped, and you could see the red beginning to climb his neck.

He must be kidding. We need to restore the engine room, and he can't even speak at a normal volume.

As I grew more impatient, the tone of my voice became more abrupt and short. "EOOW, you need to be louder."

The EOOW glanced in my direction, refusing to make eye contact. "Yes, sir," he whispered.

He directed his attention back to his watch team, slightly increasing the volume of his voice again with the red getting up to his cheeks, and said, "Watch team, report any recommendations on how to restore the engine room."

Despite the slightly higher volume, no one could understand him.

"Sir, request you say again louder," his panel operator replied.

I can't believe he won't just speak at a normal volume. How is he so paralyzed? We won't finish this drill in time to complete the last event and keep the ship on schedule.

"EOOW, you need to be louder! I cannot hear you, and I'm standing right next to you!"

The EOOW's shoulders immediately slumped further, and his face became fully flushed. "Aye, sir." His voice trembled slightly as he tried to compose himself.

He looked at his panel operator and said at the same volume, "Report any recommendations on how to restore the engine room."

"Sir, I still cannot hear you, request you say again louder."

Unbelievable.

"EOOW, turn over the watch with your assistant EOOW. You're not able to lead your team right now, and we need to recover the engine room."

"Yes, sir," the EOOW responded with complete defeat in his voice. He turned over the watch to his peer and stepped aside as the other officer began to clearly communicate and restore the engine room.

THE FEEDBACK

A day after that drill, my engineering department master chief, or EDMC, stopped by my stateroom. The EDMC is the principal enlisted advisor to the engineer officer. I trusted mine completely.

"Sir, do you have a moment to chat?"

"Of course, EDMC."

"I wanted to follow up on how that last drill went yesterday."

"I know. It was awful. I can't believe the EOOW froze the way he did."

"I'm more concerned about how the interactions went in maneuvering."

"What do you mean?"

"Well, another one of the junior officers who observed the drill came to me earlier today, concerned with the way you interacted with the EOOW. They think you were bullying him."

"What? I'm not sure what they're talking about."

"I wasn't in maneuvering, but he relayed you were just berating the EOOW and not helping him."

Wow. Could they not see how poorly he was performing? I was only trying to get him to be louder so we could recover the propulsion plant.

I paused before responding. "I don't think I was berating him. I certainly didn't intend to do that."

"Did you give him any positive feedback?"

"Well, no. I deliberately tried to minimize my talking as much as possible. I want to be able to maintain the big picture and intervene if needed. I didn't expect to need to tell someone to speak loudly enough for other people to hear him."

"Is there anything requiring you to say nothing until you're frustrated?"

Why was I waiting? What am I afraid of? I have other drill monitors present to keep the ship safe. Do I need to do that, too?

"I guess there isn't. I'm behaving how I learned from my previous engineers. I never really considered doing anything different."

"I've never been in maneuvering for drills, and I can't relate to the stress you must feel as the person responsible for safe reactor plant operations during drills. I can only tell you right now, you're losing the junior officers in your wardroom. If they don't trust that you have their best interest in mind, they won't perform."

He's right. It doesn't matter how technically correct I am or if I'm properly prioritizing plant safety if I do it in a way that ostracizes my team.

"Okay. Thanks, EDMC. I will think about what you said and change how I interact in maneuvering."

THE SUCCESS

After that conversation, I fundamentally changed how I approached behavior during drills. Moving forward, I dedicated more time to training my watch officers on expectations before drill sets. Additionally, during drills, I intervened earlier, before I became frustrated, and calmly advised them on how to succeed. Over time, this made a difference in my officers' performance, and I regained the trust I damaged with my team that day in maneuvering.

Two and a half years later, I was once again preparing my team for a fleet commander's engineering inspection. This time, I had a new group of watch officers I needed to train to succeed during casualty drills. To avoid repeating past mistakes, I applied the lessons I learned from the previous round of preparations and, more importantly, remained open to feedback from them throughout the process. I emphasized the significance of overcommunication and thinking out loud to promote watch team backup.

One particular officer was doing well in his preparations. I was pleased with his performance and expected him to be a top-performing watch officer. I was surprised when he approached me in my office one day with some concerns.

"Sir, do you have a moment to talk?"

"Of course, EA (short for electrical assistant, his divisional title), how can I help?"

"I'm really stressed out. I don't feel like I'm meeting your expectations, and I don't think I have what it takes to succeed as a watch officer."

What? How can he think he doesn't have what it takes? He is one of the best junior watch officers right now, if not the best.

"What makes you feel that way?"

"I'm constantly making mistakes in maneuvering. Sometimes I'm not immediately sure what I'm supposed to do. I'm scared I'll freeze or make one mistake too many during drills."

"Okay. A couple of things. First, I think you're doing well. You don't need to be concerned about not meeting my expectations. For your experience, you're performing above where I expect you to be.

"Second, what are the two things I taught all of you to do when you freeze or are unsure of the way forward?"

"To think out loud and overcommunicate."

"Exactly. If you think out loud to your watch team, they know what you believe to be the way forward. They can either reinforce you're correct or back you up and redirect you. If you then overcommunicate your plan and encourage your panel operators to do the same thing, you'll all be on the same page.

"I don't expect individual perfection. I expect team excellence. At any time, you or your panel operators could make an individual mistake. As long as you think out loud and overcommunicate, then you'll succeed as a team by being present for each other."

His shoulders relaxed as if a weight lifted. "Thank you, sir. I was sure I wasn't going to make it."

"You have nothing to worry about. You're on track and doing well."

A month later, the inspection team arrived. As we expected, he was chosen to lead one of the drills. This time around, the drills were occurring in a trainer, and I wouldn't be in maneuvering with him. He was all by himself with only his team to rely on.

As the drill commenced, a spurious alarm came in as a planned distraction to see what his team would do before the drill began. His panel operator's first reaction was to take early action before recognizing which casualty was in progress.

"EOOW, taking my first immediate action for improper steam plant chemistry!"

Oh no! They're about to go down the wrong path!

"Wait! We don't have all the correct indications yet."

Phew!

"Wait, aye, sir." The panel operator sat back down and backed away from taking his immediate action.

Suddenly, a loud rushing noise filled the room. The drill started. Because of the noise, I could no longer hear the interactions, but what I observed was impressive. The deafening sound made it impossible for his watch team to hear him when he spoke at a normal volume. To tackle this challenge, he moved quickly between his three panel operators, providing direction, communicating his observations, and thinking out loud.

Over the course of the next thirty minutes, the watch team performed excellently. They protected each other from individual mistakes and took all actions correctly.

When the drill was over, the senior inspector looked at me and said, "That was nuclear nirvana."

At that moment, I could not have been prouder. Watching the EA succeed by himself is one of the most powerful memories of my career.

THE STRATEGY

Upon reflection, I learned the importance of establishing a relationship built on trust as a prerequisite for any leader-follower or mentor-mentee interactions. Once this trust is established, overcommunicating clear expectations and adjusting them based on feedback from your team fosters a shared commitment. Lastly, the team must understand the personal or professional consequences of failing to uphold this shared commitment.

I continue to apply these lessons to both leadership and mentorship interactions. Surprisingly, I find it more challenging to establish a relationship of empathetic accountability in a mentor-mentee relationship than in a leader-follower relationship. Without the natural lines of accountability present in a leader-follower relationship, a mentor must rely on the strength of their personal relationship with the mentee to hold them accountable for meeting their goals.

My EDMC set an example for me by holding me accountable for my poor behavior in maneuvering. We had an established relationship of trust where I knew he had my best interests in mind. Although he could not directly relate to my experience, he empathized with my position and the pressure I felt at the time. He provided me with clear feedback and communicated a real consequence if I did not change.

This example provides the framework for the elements of empathetic accountability.

1. Establish a relationship of trust.

Before you can truly hold someone accountable, they must know who you are. People reveal their true selves through their actions, not their words. Many mentors claim to care about their mentees, yet they often know little about their personal lives. Building trust involves being vulnerable. Be present for your mentee by making yourself available to them whenever they need you.

2. Empathize with the mentee's perspective.

Take the time to put yourself in your mentee's position. By listening to and understanding their perspective, you can ask the right questions to guide them in achieving their goals and improving.

3. Establish a shared commitment.

Clearly communicate your time and capability boundaries. Once your mentee identifies the areas they want to improve, encourage them to set measurable goals with clear deadlines to follow up with you as their mentor. When the mentee takes ownership of this shared commitment's parameters, they're more likely to succeed. Equally important, this groundwork allows a mentor to ensure their mentee follows through on their goals.

4. Provide clear feedback.

This element is the most important. A mentor cannot simply agree with the mentee and be a superficial sounding board. Challenge the mentee to broaden their perspective. Ask thought-provoking questions and spend more time listening than speaking. Encourage them to step out of their comfort zone and honestly reflect on their shortcomings and opportunities for growth.

5. Identify the tangible consequence.

Effectively communicating the consequences of failing to implement necessary changes is often the key to growth. This may require time and posing challenging questions to help the mentee realize the implications for them. Once the mentee understands these consequences, they can begin to make progress. In addition to clarifying the consequences of failing to change for their personal growth, make sure to communicate the repercussions if they fail to honor time commitments with you as the mentor.

Using the empathetic accountability framework outlined above establishes a foundation for mentors to help mentees achieve their goals. This approach allows for objective discussions about progress. If any of the aforementioned elements are absent, accountability becomes impossible.

Without trust, the mentee will struggle to be vulnerable. If the mentor fails to invest time in understanding the mentee, their perspective will be skewed by personal experience. Absence of a shared commitment from the mentee puts the mentor at risk of guiding them in an incorrect direction or, worse, creating frustration and ineffectiveness by not fully grasping the desired outcomes of the relationship. Without clear, honest feedback, mentors risk letting mentees stagnate or neglect necessary changes. Finally, without recognizing the consequences, mentees will lack the motivation needed for sustainable improvement.

Empathetic accountability means following through on a shared commitment built on a relationship of trust.

CDR **James Montgomery**, U.S. Navy, is a career submariner who has completed three tours of duty on submarines, during which he conducted two under-ice deployments to the Arctic Circle and three strategic deterrent patrols. He currently serves as the commanding officer of Moored Training Ship 711 San Francisco in Charleston, South Carolina.

James attended the United States Naval Academy, graduating with merit with a B.S. in mechanical engineering in May 2009. He later earned an M.A. in leadership, education, and development from George Washington University in May 2015.

James's growth as a mentor began when he served as a company officer at the United States Naval Academy from 2015 to 2017. During this period, he led and mentored over 300 future officers in the Navy and Marine Corps. In 2016, he completed a leadership fellowship with the Severn Leadership Group and incorporates their philosophy of virtuous leadership to enhance his moral foundation, which is rooted in Jesuit philosophy from his time at Saint Xavier High School in Cincinnati, Ohio.

The Severn Leadership Group certified James as one of their senior mentors in 2020. Through this organization, he volunteers his time to guide mid-career professionals to improve their leadership skills and lead with virtue.

James is married to the former Kambridge Emde of Charleston, South Carolina. They have one daughter, Anna Kathleen, and currently reside in Summerville, South Carolina.

Connect with James:

Facebook: https://www.facebook.com/james.b.montgomery

LinkedIn: https://www.linkedin.com/in/james-montgomery-29ab5a43/

CHAPTER TWENTY-THREE

TEAMWORK, TONE, TENACITY

LEADERSHIP PILLARS
THAT MAKE AN IMPACT

Rear Admiral Paul Becker, U.S. Navy (Ret.)

MY STORY

I thought my career was over.

It was midday at sea, steaming off the southern California coast in early October 2001. That morning, I was confident in my work and looked forward to the evening's baseball playoff games after a busy day afloat. Suddenly, that afternoon, I contemplated an earlier-than-expected retirement from the Navy.

Instead of preparing for combat in the Middle East in the aftermath of 9/11 as a Naval intelligence commander with the aircraft carrier USS John C. Stennis (CVN 74), I faced the possibility of sitting this conflict out as an observer at home because of a failed pre-deployment certification exam.

Professionally, the news couldn't be any worse. The scores I received from my evaluator stunned every officer in the shipboard conference room, especially my admiral. The harsh assessment indicated: "Significant problems noted … [this group is] not ready for a combat deployment."

While those PowerPoint words hovered over the conference room like a dense Southern California fog, some of my fellow officers started moving their seats to put distance between us along the steel bulkhead of our cramped shipboard compartment. It was easy to determine who your friends were in such circumstances. I had seemingly become toxic.

No need to sit next to this under-performer, others may have thought. We need to prepare for a combat deployment quickly, and this new guy will only slow us down.

Allow me to roll back the clock a few weeks to better set the scene. America was viciously and surprisingly attacked by terrorists several weeks earlier on a fateful September day in 2001. Like many, I lost close friends—John and Joe Vigiano, one FDNY and one NYPD officer—in Manhattan, and shipmates—Lieutenant Commander Vince Tolbert and Lieutenant Darin Pontell—in the Pentagon. I wanted a chance to deliver justice to their memories. A short-notice deployment with our aircraft carrier USS John C. Stennis (CNV-74) was the way to do this. Certification for the entire sea-going team, including the intelligence department, was required before we steamed toward the setting sun and the Middle East.

I just reported to Stennis in late August. My wife and I were still unpacking moving boxes in our Coronado townhome on the morning of 9/11. I was new to the equipment, new to my shipmates, and new to the San Diego waterfront. Additionally, I was rusty on the tactics, techniques, and procedures required to maximize the intelligence tools at our disposal, demonstrating success and uncovering what the enemy didn't want us to know.

With that background, it's not surprising we failed our exam. The accountability and responsibility for the equipment and team members' performance were mine and mine alone. After the evaluation meeting concluded and the room started clearing out, my boss, Rear Admiral Jim "Zorro" Zortman, came toward me as everyone else moved away.

"That was a terrible evaluation, Paul."

"Yessir," I ashamedly replied.

"Do you have what it takes to fix it before we deploy in a few weeks?" he asked.

"Yes," I replied, more confidently this time.

"What can you offer to improve the team?" the admiral inquired.

"Teamwork, tone, tenacity," I responded.

"Good," said Zorro with a smile. We knew each other, and earlier in our careers, I earned his trust through a solid work ethic and demonstrations of integrity. "Well then, you better get after it. You've got a lot of work to do before we deploy next month, and you're coming with us as our intelligence officer."

With that, the admiral declared to me and the rest of the staff that he had confidence in my ability to apply these three pillars of leadership to improve our intelligence team's performance and productivity—and get us ready for war.

Admiral Zortman taught me an invaluable lesson about leadership that afternoon. Even though I failed at a particular task, he didn't make me feel like a failure. When others lost confidence in me and put distance between us, he maintained confidence and drew closer to mentor me and provide support when I needed it most. That was a demonstration of empathy and trust I rarely found in my professional career, and a memory and feeling I will always carry with me.

Like a good mentor, instead of telling me what to do, he also tacitly endorsed my strategic leadership pillars—teamwork, tone, and tenacity—through which I achieved outstanding workplace results over time.

THE STRATEGY

Our team failed the inspection for many reasons that October day. Lack of unified purpose, unnecessary displays of emotion, absence of trust, and no demonstration of perseverance were just a few of them. With 18 years of Navy experience up to that point, I recognized from previous leadership predicaments what the root causes of failure were here. More importantly, I realized what needed to be done to turn this travail into triumph.

For years, I diligently journaled in my government-issued, ugly, bright green, cloth-covered five-by-eight-inch division officer notebook. Now it was time to put all these observations to the test.

I started journaling and highlighting the attributes of military leaders in those notebooks in 1983. By 2001, the stack of them stood about two feet tall. Along the way, I wrote about many leadership styles. Some were good. Some were great. Some were terrible! After my first few deployments and shore assignments, it was clear that the best leaders who stood apart from the pack were the most inclusive, compassionate, self-aware, good-natured, common-sensical, and resolute. That led me to wonder: What's the difference between a good and a great leader? It boiled down to three defining traits: teamwork, tone, and tenacity.

Why just three? Many lists highlight positive leadership traits and actions that help make people and organizations great. For example, Marcus Aurelius' *Meditations* references ten rules for being an exceptional leader. The late retired Army General Colin Powell had "13 Rules of Leadership." John Maxwell authored the bestselling book *21 Irrefutable Laws of Leadership*. So why are teamwork, tone, and tenacity worth focusing on?

These three attributes form a superior set of mutually reinforcing behaviors aimed at meeting the mission, taking care of people, and developing subordinates. They also fit together well in a short, actionable, memorable phrase. Aurelius, Powell, Maxwell, and others offer valuable advice, but that advice takes time to recall and apply.

"Teamwork, tone, tenacity" is user-ready in the fast-paced, LinkedIn-looking, Facebook-friending, X-tuned, information-intensive environment in which military and civilian leaders operate today. The guidance is immediately retrievable because it focuses on intent instead of tasks. Additionally, cognitive skill research indicates human minds are well conditioned to remember directions and phrases that flow in sets of three: "lights, camera, action," "ready, aim, fire," "duty, honor, country." Now, add to them "teamwork, tone, tenacity."

Leaders and followers can recall and execute specific practices associated with "teamwork, tone, tenacity" rapidly in any situation, from a contested combat zone to a boisterous board room. Knowing and understanding a leader's clear, actionable, memorable guidance—commander's intent—greatly increases the chances of success in those seeking to achieve a common goal.

TEAMWORK

Teamwork doesn't come naturally; it needs to be taught. It begins by building trust.

A leader has many responsibilities, and one of the most important is building relationships. The result of relationships is trust, and the byproduct of trust is loyalty. Loyalty to the team is the essence of workplace morale, whether wearing a uniform or a business suit. The culture of teamwork was, and is, imbued in the organization from the top.

The best military teams I ever encountered were led by officers who established a command climate where trust and loyalty between every echelon and member of the team were the norm and where every teammate understood what needed to be accomplished. Teamwork is often best described by the maritime maxim, which prioritizes focus, loyalty, and effort on "ship, shipmate, self."

Improving yourself is the building block of an organization. Shipmate is the willingness to sacrifice for a fellow member of the team. Ship is a relentless focus on mission and achieving common goals.

To ensure the teams I was part of understood our mission and goals, I printed and distributed a simple trifold document, most often on gold paper, and it became known as "The Gold Standard." It had panels that characterized our operating environment, why we did what we did, what we did, and how we did it. This reinforced the constants. It maintained focus and a shared understanding of common goals.

Teamwork also proves especially important when two parties disagree on an issue because it gives you something to fall back on. Knowing the character of the individual you're working with prevents a professional relationship from devolving into accusatory discourse and incivility. This lesson can be applied well elsewhere in today's society.

TONE

There are a lot of dimensions to tone. When I reflect on leaders who demonstrate it best, I recall their positive attitudes, which caused a chain reaction of positive thoughts, events, and outcomes. I valued leaders who were genuine, whose words matched their deeds (integrity), and who were willing to take the time to teach and train. They were always comfortable with who they were and not afraid to accept risk for morally courageous choices.

When they asked, "How are you doing?" they meant it and were ready to listen to a real response. When asked, "What's the right thing to do here?" they explained their answer to everyone the choice impacted. If someone wrote the leader of a high-performing organization, you could count on that leader replying in a timely fashion to demonstrate they valued others' time and effort and display that responsiveness equals respect!

Tone also applies to maintaining an advantage over a crisis by remaining cool and unruffled. A good tone creates a positive command climate that makes people want to come to work and excel every day.

TENACITY

I like Thomas Edison's quote: "Genius is one percent inspiration and 99% perspiration." There's no substitute for the hard work it takes to understand all aspects of an issue, being involved and visible to your people, communicating standards, and ensuring all members of the organization understand the objective and how to implement a solution. The most tenacious leaders I ever served with were junior to me and provided me with a healthy dose of junior subordinate reverse mentoring.

I think back to when teams I was on suffered setbacks and were in organizational disarray. It was some of the junior and non-commissioned officers who placed tackling and solving our toughest unit problems ahead of their comfort and ambition. They demonstrated endurance in a hostile environment, but also persistence with a purpose and a relentless focus, combined with certainty of what would transpire. For these tireless patriots, failure was never a permanent option, just a temporary obstacle.

In summary, "teamwork, tone, tenacity" is easy to recognize, easy to remember, and easy to apply. I'm fortunate to have benefited from seeing these attributes personified by outstanding warriors and leaders across several decades in peace, crisis, and combat. Together, they comprise pillars of leadership that make an impact for today's leaders in the military, public, and private sectors.

Rear Admiral **Paul Becker**, U.S. Navy (Ret.), is a motivational keynote speaker. He served for 30 years around the world, afloat and ashore. Paul is a leadership professor at the U.S. Naval Academy and a certified executive coach.

Rear Admiral Becker is the recipient of the National Intelligence Community and Department of Defense's Distinguished Service Medals, the Navy's Distinguished Service Medal, and the Ellis Island Medal of Honor. Specific military service includes: the Director of Intelligence (J2) for the Joint Chiefs of Staff, where he was the principal intelligence and cybersecurity advisor to the chairman, the U.S. Pacific Command in Hawaii, and the International Security Assistance Force Joint Command in Afghanistan.

Paul is president of a nonprofit board: the U.S. Naval Academy's Friends of the Jewish Chapel. He's a member of several boards of advisors and a long-time volunteer mentor with The Severn Leadership Group. He holds a master's in public administration from Harvard's Kennedy School of Government and a Bachelor of Science from the U.S. Naval Academy.

A dynamic public speaker and author, his articles and presentations have been widely published. In 2016, The Naval Intelligence Community established The Rear Admiral Becker's Teamwork, Tone, Tenacity Award for Leadership in his honor.

Connect with Paul:

Website: https://TheBeckerT3Group.com

CHAPTER TWENTY-FOUR

COACHING VS. MENTORING

KNOWING THE DIFFERENCE, HONORING THE IMPACT

AliceAnne Loftus, Leadership and Business Coach

MY STORY

Over the years, I've been called both a coach and a mentor, sometimes in the same conversation, sometimes in the same sentence. While I consider both roles an honor, I've learned they're not the same. Understanding the distinction has changed the way I lead, support, and show up in every relationship I hold.

After nearly a decade of coaching women in leadership and business, and mentoring women through the Leading Lady community. I began noticing the subtle but significant differences between the two roles. As a coach, I'm often hired for strategy, structure, and accountability. As a mentor, I'm invited to hold space, share my own experiences, offer perspective, and remind others they're not alone.

That distinction became even clearer in 2024 when I participated as a Fellow in the Severn Leadership Group's mentoring program. There was no performance to track, no metric to measure. Instead, I was given space.

Space to reflect. To process. To be heard without urgency. My mentor didn't hand me a plan or outline a next step. She listened. She asked thoughtful questions. She shared her own story, not to direct me, but to show me I wasn't alone. Going through that experience showed me the differences in such a profound way. It also highlighted to me why we need to not only know the difference between coaching and mentoring, but we also need to honor the impact of how each role supports a person, an organization, and a community. When we don't clarify which role we're stepping into, it can lead to miscommunication, unmet expectations, and unclear boundaries, for both the person offering support and the one receiving it.

In this chapter, I'll explore how to recognize the difference between coaching and mentoring, why it matters, and how to step into each role with confidence. Whether you're supporting a friend, leading a team, or growing a community, understanding this distinction will help you lead with greater clarity and care. While coaching and mentoring are both powerful forms of support, they serve different purposes. Mentoring is about *who you are becoming*, guided by someone who has walked a similar path. Coaching is about *what you want to achieve*, supported by someone trained to help you navigate that journey. If you've ever wondered which role you're stepping into, or felt unclear about what's being asked of you, this chapter will give you the language, clarity, and a framework for showing up with purpose.

HERE'S WHY MAKING THE DISTINCTION MATTERS

Coaching is a structured relationship designed to help someone reach a specific goal. Mentoring, on the other hand, is often more organic, it's about walking alongside someone and sharing the wisdom you've gained from your own journey. Both are powerful. Both can be life-changing. However, when we don't know the difference, we risk showing up in a way that doesn't truly serve the person in front of us.

1. Expectations Can Be Unclear

Clarity isn't just a nice-to-have; it's foundational to trust, progress, and feeling truly supported. When we blur the lines between coaching and mentoring, even with the best of intentions, expectations can get murky, and relationships can suffer for it.

A person might come to you for personal wisdom and encouragement, expecting mentorship, but you begin goal-setting and accountability work, like a coach. The alternative is that someone might want a focused strategy and outcomes, but receives unstructured storytelling and emotional support. When expectations don't match the style of support, both people can feel uncertain or disappointed, even when the intention is good.

Early in my coaching journey, I ran into this dynamic more than once. I'm a natural problem-solver. My instinct is to take action when someone shares a challenge with me. I shift into strategy mode fast. That's where I shine. Despite these skills, I started to notice moments when a client wasn't ready for strategy. They were still processing the *story* of the problem, needing to be heard, to sit with it a bit longer. I wasn't giving them what they needed, and they weren't wrong to want it. We just hadn't identified the true guidelines and objectives of what they needed and what I offered.

Some clients told me I had a "tough love" approach or that I didn't do a lot of cheerleading. At first, that stung. *What do they mean!? I care deeply. I'm compassionate. I am cheering for them!* I tried to defend my intentions. As a coach, I hold high expectations and a forward-focused mindset. If a client came back repeatedly without following through on the goals we set, I found myself asking them:

"Do you need me to be a sounding board right now, or are we still committed to the strategy we outlined together?"

That question helped me discern what *they* needed and whether I was the right person to support them in that season.

2. Boundaries Get Blurry

Each role carries different assumptions about time, compensation, and emotional availability. Coaching is often professional and structured. Mentoring is often relational and informal. If those lines aren't clear, it can create confusion about what's being offered. Clarifying your role helps you show up fully without overextending or underdelivering.

I remember the first time I worked with a mentor instead of hiring a coach. It felt weird. I wasn't paying her. There were no scheduled calls. No outcomes. Just a kind, experienced woman who offered to walk with me.

And yet, every time I wanted to message her, I hesitated.

Am I bothering her?

Does she really have time for this?

I'm just venting; I shouldn't take up her energy.

Guilt and uncertainty crept in because I didn't fully understand the nature of the relationship. It didn't feel like a transaction, but I didn't know how to navigate it as a connection. She had to remind me, more than once, "I *want* to hold space for you. I *offered* to mentor you. It's not a burden!"

As we continued, something even more surprising happened: her listening became the support. She didn't offer solutions. She didn't give me a plan. She didn't map out action steps. At first, that threw me off. As a coach, I'm trained for momentum. I love clarity. I thrive in goal-setting and next steps. But this? This was slow. Open. Reflective. She stayed steady in her boundary, not to fix me, but to witness me.

At one point, just as I was ready to give up on the whole dynamic, she said something simple:

"I've actually been through something similar."

That changed everything.

She wasn't trying to teach me. She was simply showing me I wasn't alone. Suddenly, that was enough. Having someone hold space for my story, without agenda or urgency, was deeply unfamiliar. It became profoundly comforting. There was no pressure to justify how I felt, no race to move through it, just space—safe, intentional space.

Honestly, if she had blurred that boundary and tried to coach me through it, I would've missed the deeper gift of mentorship altogether.

This ties right into my next point:

3. The Right Support Might Not Be Delivered

Even with the best intentions, offering the wrong kind of support can miss the mark. A mentor might share a personal story when what's truly needed is a clear path forward. A coach might deliver a framework when what's really needed is compassionate space to process. Being mindful of what kind of support is needed and what role you're stepping into allows you to respond with greater clarity and care.

As I shared earlier, the mentor I worked with knew her role. She didn't try to coach me through my struggle or push me toward action when what I needed was space, reflection, and understanding. That clarity created safety.

On the flip side, if someone is actively seeking a plan and only receives empathy or shared experience, without any tangible steps, it can feel frustrating or unhelpful, even if the intention was kind.

That's why I believe it's essential to name the role early on. When someone shares a challenge with me in a coaching container, they know they'll receive strategy, structure, and solution-focused support. Just as I appreciated when my mentor chose to hold space instead of rushing me toward a plan, I know my clients value the clarity that comes with knowing what kind of support they'll receive from me. The power isn't just in the support itself; it's in offering the *right* support, at the *right* time, in the *right* way.

4. Mutual Trust and Growth Depend on Clarity

When both people understand the nature of the relationship, whether it's coaching, mentoring, or a thoughtful mix of both (which can be done beautifully!), they're more likely to feel safe, respected, and empowered. That clarity becomes a container for growth. It's not about labeling one role as better than the other. It's about being intentional and honest about how you're showing up. When the lines are blurred, assumptions take over. One person might expect guidance, while the other is prepared to simply listen. One might anticipate accountability and deliverables, while the other shows up to share experience and empathy. However, when roles are defined from the start, the support becomes cleaner, more effective, and more liberating. Both people know what to expect and how to engage. That mutual understanding builds trust, fosters alignment, and helps the relationship thrive without unnecessary tension or confusion.

Clarity creates safety.

Safety creates trust.

Trust creates transformation.

When we step into a support role, whether as coach, mentor, or something in between, our greatest gift is presence. Having said that, presence without clarity can create confusion. By simply naming the role and aligning our approach with what's truly needed, we elevate our impact, honor our boundaries, and deepen the trust that makes growth possible.

So the goal isn't to box yourself in. It's to show up with purpose. Here are some questions to ask yourself:

- What does this person need from me?
- What capacity do I have to support them?
- Are we both clear on the kind of relationship we're in?

Naming the role doesn't limit the connection, it strengthens it. Let's go a little deeper with an exercise and strategy tool to help you get clarity on the mentorship and coaching roles.

THE STRATEGY

Mentorship & Coaching Role Clarity

Use this tool before entering a support conversation, starting a client relationship, or offering help to someone in your community. It's designed to help you pause, reflect, and lead with clarity.

THE ROLE CLARITY REFLECTION:

"Am I Coaching, Mentoring, or Something In Between?"

Step 1: What's Being Asked of Me?

Ask yourself:

- Is this person looking for strategy and structure, or shared experience and support?
- Do they want guidance through a defined challenge, or a relationship to grow alongside?
- Are they seeking accountability and results, or wisdom and reflection?

☐ Primarily Coaching

☐ Primarily Mentoring

☐ A Blend (but which do they *need most* right now?)

Step 2: What Capacity Am I In?

Check in with your own role and boundaries:

- Am I being paid or professionally engaged for this conversation?
- Am I here with time-limited focus, or open-ended presence?
- Do I feel equipped to offer the support they're asking for?

☐ I'm in a Coaching role

☐ I'm in a Mentoring role

☐ I need to clarify before continuing

Step 3: Start with Clarity

Here are simple, permission-giving phrases to define your role:

If you're coaching:

"I'm here to help you move forward with a clear strategy. Let's define what success looks like and build a plan together."

If you're mentoring:

"I'm here to walk with you through this. I've had a similar experience, and I'd be happy to share what helped me."

If you're unsure:

"Before we dive in, what kind of support feels most helpful to you right now?"

Final Reflection:

When I know what's needed and what I'm able to offer, I serve better. I don't have to be everything; I just have to be clear.

AliceAnne Loftus is a leadership and business coach, community builder, and mentorship advocate dedicated to helping women lead with clarity, confidence, and connection. As the founder of Leading Lady Coaching, she has spent nearly a decade coaching high-achieving women and mentoring entrepreneurs through thoughtfully curated communities that prioritize both personal growth and professional excellence. Her mission is rooted in the belief that women are most powerful when they rise together. Through her work, she helps women ditch perfectionism, rediscover their voice, and build businesses and lives aligned with their deepest values. She is the creator of The Leading Lady Collective, a vibrant in-person networking group in Annapolis, Maryland, and The Leading Lady Business Hub, an online platform offering weekly coaching, expert resources, and a supportive global community.

AliceAnne is also the author of *Take the Lead* and the *We Lead* book series, where she shares stories of resilience, vision, and leadership from women across industries. Her leadership style is honest, evolving, and deeply influenced by her faith, love of learning, and dedication to excellence.

As a mentor and coach, AliceAnne is known for her warm presence, practical wisdom, and ability to see the potential in others before they see it in themselves. Whether she's hosting a leadership workshop, mentoring a business owner, or sharing her story on stage, her goal is always the same: to help women rise in wisdom and build with joy.

AliceAnne lives in Annapolis with her husband, their two young adult children, and her beloved dog, Scout. When she's not coaching or speaking, you'll find her cooking for family and friends, arranging fresh flowers, or enjoying a quiet morning with coffee and a journal.

Connect with AliceAnne:

Website: https://www.leadinglady-coaching.com

Instagram: https://www.instagram.com/leading.lady.coach

Facebook: https://www.facebook.com/groups/LeadingLadiesAAL

LinkedIn: https://www.linkedin.com/in/aliceanne-loftus-cpc-eli-mp-22323911a/

CHAPTER TWENTY-FIVE

NOT A CLOSING

A NEW BEGINNING

Julie Campbell, President/CEO, Severn Leadership Group

For the last few years, I've pondered how I could bottle all of the amazing wisdom from our SLG Mentors. I've been blessed to participate as a co-author in other collaborative books masterfully guided by Laura Di Franco. I presented this option to a small team of people I consider my mentors (Bruce Engelhardt, Judy Farrell, and Renee Sherwood) and received excited "yesses" and a willingness to help me plan, gain interest, and most importantly, write a chapter!

All of our authors have led teams. All have been mentored. All continue to mentor today. These mentors get the highest ratings in our programs. Every single mentor-author has had a profound impact on my life.

This is an esteemed group of brothers, sisters, and good friends. They understand the value of seeking outside perspectives; that it is a sign of strength (not weakness) and commitment to others. They understand the importance of virtue in leadership, mentorship, and life, and they live it every day.

In the work that we do, I get to watch this beautiful symphony of multi-generational, multi-industry leadership mentoring unfold. Nothing is more fulfilling than seeing a flourishing mentor-mentee relationship. And it is especially fun and enlightening to witness reverse-mentoring when a mentor learns life lessons from their mentee. There is measurable growth for both mentor and mentee.

Mentoring begins by building a healthy relationship.

From the moment we met, I knew this was going to be a meaningful relationship. My mentor provided a safe space where I could be honest and vulnerable. She shared her successes and failures, allowing me to learn and grow from her experiences. Her insights and practical advice were immediately applicable. In a short time, she contributed exponentially to my growth. I'm truly grateful.

~ SLG Fellow

These mentors build trust and go deep after only 1-2 sessions with their mentees. They literally "walk" alongside their mentees during hikes, bike rides, meals, fishing, and even pedicures, as they live their leadership journey together.

In this book, you get just a glimpse of how our mentors make a difference in another's life, through their authentic, courageous, and powerful stories. It's more than a collection of "sea stories". It's a community of hope.

Their story is our story.

At every Fellows Program commencement, we emphasize that this is not the end, but a new beginning.

This collection reflects that journey. It's never too late to start mentoring. It's never too late to add to your mentor tool bag. It's never too late to be mentored.

The world needs more mentors. Who are you walking alongside?

Remember my mentor Brian from Chapter 1? It was not until I reconnected with Brian, years later, that he shared:

"From my perspective … at the core of mentorship is **gratitude** for one's life's blessings … and at my core … a belief the Good Lord has placed the person in your life to be the channel of the Lord's love to the person you are mentoring."

Nudged by his faith, he further related: "But in all reality … humility would require me to say the words are those of the Holy Spirit to each one of us."

May this book be the nudge you need to be the mentor you are called to be.

ACKNOWLEDGEMENTS

To the SLG Mentors who took the leap and offered to write a chapter in this one-of-a-kind book, thank you! This was a BIG project during seasons of overwhelming busyness, yet you set aside your precious time to share your wisdom with vulnerability and practical steps to help others mentor holistically and mentor well.

Sig Berg, your vision for the Severn Leadership Group, where virtues, not values, are the key to building leaders of character, and a systems approach to leadership, followership, and mentorship, has changed my life and the lives of countless others. Thank you for having the courage to launch SLG and for your mentorship over the last 10 years.

Early in our journey, we had the privilege of having deep conversations on mentoring with Rick Woolworth and Jane Grizzle from Telemachus. This mentor-mentee team was a beacon of holistic mentoring, encouraging and confirming that we were headed in the right direction. Rick left this world too soon, but his memory lives on in the mentoring that we do.

Sometimes we employ mentor pods in our work, where two to three fellows are assigned to one mentor. The 1:1 session is amplified as 3-4 intertwine in the mentor pod, a natural small group, where learning is amplified. This is due in part to what I've learned during my time as a fellow with the C. S. Lewis Institute, under the wise and welcoming leadership of Rob Shepherd, a co-author of this book. Rob has been one of my biggest cheerleaders and rocks when I've aspired to try something different. He's always there with an affirming word and a welcoming hug. Rob, you are an extraordinary example of a virtuous leader and mentor.

Laura Di Franco and the team at Brave Healer Productions, thank you for your rock-solid guidance, patience, and expertise. You have made the stories from this diverse team of professionals, engineers, past and present military members, pastors, and old and new friends into a powerful and endearing collection of goodness that will change the world through mentoring.

To Codie Seier, the lady behind the scenes: without your organization, gentle yet persistent follow-up, and brilliant feedback, I would not have been able to pursue such a monumental project while keeping all of the other balls we are juggling in the air.

Finally, to my husband, Chris, and my boys, Mark and Luke. Thank you for your understanding when Mom has to (and wants to) work. You are still the why behind what I do. You love the SLG Mentors as much as I do, and your willingness to pause and your patience when Mom takes another call from an SLG Mentor are truly appreciated.

Invest in your leadership journey and become an SLG Fellow

https://www.severnleadership.org/fellows-program

Become an SLG Mentor

https://www.severnleadership.org/mentors-program

Strengthen your team and fortify your organization's culture

https://www.severnleadership.org/teams-program

Learn more about the why and how of SLG with

The Virtue Proposition: Five Virtues That Will Transform Leadership, Team Performance, and You by Sig Berg

https://virtueproposition.com/

A sign of a good leader is not how many followers you have, but how many leaders you create.

~ Mahatma Gandhi

www.ingramcontent.com/pod-product-compliance
Lightning Source LLC
Chambersburg PA
CBHW071547210326
41597CB00019B/3149